Safe $ex
on
Wall
Street

Safe $ex on Wall Street

Van William Knox III   Peter J. DeAngelis, CFA

CB
CONTEMPORARY
BOOKS
CHICAGO

Library of Congress Cataloging-in-Publication Data

Knox, Van William.
    Safe $ex on Wall Street : the prudent investor's guide to
making money in the market / Van William Knox III and
Peter J. DeAngelis : illustrations by Kieran Vogel.
       p.   cm.
    ISBN 0-8092-3898-5 (paper)
    1. Investments.   I. DeAngelis, Peter J.   II. Title.
III. Title: Safe sex on Wall Street.
HG4521.K574   1992
332.6—dc20   92-13795
                                                         CIP

Published by Contemporary Books, Inc.
180 North Michigan Avenue, Chicago, Illinois 60601
Manufactured in the United States of America
International Standard Book Number: 0-8092-3898-5

Contents

Preface

The two of us were finally sitting down over a pizza. We had recently completed, in collaboration with several other investment professionals, a large and quite serious book on investing and were trying to agree on a title for it. As increasingly large chunks of pizza were washed down with comparably increasing amounts of our favorite brew, the suggested titles became at once less reverent, less appropriate, and less likely. One such suggestion, however—*Safe Sex on Wall Street*—just wouldn't quite go away, no matter how wrong we agreed it would be for the book just finished . . . which was, after all, a *studious* book. Nevertheless, the germ of the idea—a light-handed presentation of perfectly valid investment techniques, taking advantage of remarkable parallels in the two types of activities and in the terms commonly used to describe both—was born.

Our enthusiasm has grown as the outline has matured and developed into text. In the presentation of our material in this humorous vein, we were greatly aided by the extremely talented young cartoonist, Kieran Vogel, whose original material appears in this book, with a contribution from his protégé, Matthew DeAngelis.

We have had a lot of fun with *Safe Sex on Wall Street.* We hope you, the reader, will, too—and that you may find among its dictums the nuggets of wisdom that will lead to your highest degree of investing comfort, satisfaction, and pleasure!

Safe $ex
on
Wall
Street

1
Foreplay
(Warming Up to Take the Plunge)

Psychologists who devote their professional careers to the study of sex (yes, they really are called sexologists)—from Kinsey in the 1950s, to Masters and Johnson in the early 1970s, all the way to Dr. Ruth today—stress the importance of *foreplay* in achieving the best possible results in a sexual encounter. Not only is it gratifying by itself, but, according to the experts, foreplay has a direct bearing on just how good you feel about "the act" itself.

Think about this: achieving success in the investment area requires exactly the same kinds of skills, the same level of preparation, and many of the same techniques. How you get ready for the process of investing, and how you lead up to the act of investing itself, will have a tremendous impact on the degree of satisfaction you achieve.

Visualize the perfect dream sequence with a perfect date. You spend considerable time and effort establishing a romantic background complete with the right music, the right lighting, the right food and drink. You make sure there will be no unwanted interruptions or intrusions. You review all you know about the object of your affections to ensure a smooth and easy time together that will lead to ever-increasing levels of excitement and pleasure and a fantastic sense of well-being as the evening progresses, culminating in an explosion of delight and a warm glow of mutual admiration. Preparation, you are sure, will pay off!

Believe it or not, the most sophisticated and successful Wall Streeters approach their investment "dating" in exactly the same way. And the time they spend *before* they start to issue buy or sell orders makes a formidable difference in how well they actually do in the market.

The first step toward becoming the Rudolph Valentino or the Mae West of your local investment scene involves the kind of behind-the-scenes preparation that, when successfully undertaken, will never even be apparent on the surface. It means taking a good, hard look at yourself and figuring out what is most appealing about your approach (things to stress) as well as what is least appealing (things to hide, if you cannot change them).

First question: Is your life sufficiently in order for you to get into this in the first place? In interpersonal terms, are you really ready for a serious relationship, given the level of chaos of everything else in your life? For the potential investor, this question means making sure that your immediate financial requirements have already been met before you decide to jump into the investment markets. Have you reviewed your insurance and are you properly covered? Do you have sufficient funds set aside in a very liquid vehicle (e.g., money market account or savings account) to meet any reasonably anticipated needs? Is your debt situation under control (not only in terms of a mortgage on the house

but in terms of your credit card balances and installment commitments)? Getting the rest of your financial
life in order before you get into the investment game is
absolutely essential for two very important reasons: you
need to be able to concentrate on your investments
with the least possible distraction from other financial
preoccupations, and you should never commit money
to an investment program if you are going to need that
money for something else in the relatively near future.
Timing the market is so difficult under the best of
circumstances that you simply cannot afford to ignore
the possibility that *any* investment may go down in the
very short run—for reasons that may have nothing to
do with its ultimate potential for success. Trying to
invest next month's rent money is likely to lead to an
uncomfortable existence with no roof over your head!

Next question: Are you emotionally and psycholog-
ically equipped to deal with the inevitable significant
swings—and possibly even losses—that will occur? Nobody goes into a relationship (whether a romantic liaison or an infatuation with a hot technology stock)
expecting that it will *not* work out. Nevertheless things
don't always turn out to be what they may at first have
appeared, and it behooves every would-be investor to
consider just how he or she will react when "making
out" turns into "breaking up." Although investing is not
gambling, it is wise in either case to consider ahead of
time how much you can afford to lose and how hard it
will be on you if you lose it.

One more question you need to ask before taking
the plunge: What kind of commitment are you prepared to make? Are you looking for a quick thrill or the
possibility of a lifelong connection? How much of yourself—your time and effort, your resources, and your
emotional energy—are you prepared to put into this?
There are many different levels of satisfaction and many

different *kinds* of satisfaction in a romance, depending upon the needs and desires of the participants—just as there are many different objectives that are valid within an investment program. Part of the secret of success, both in love and on Wall Street, lies in figuring out ahead of time exactly what you are after! Different goals require different kinds of partners . . . not to make too delicate a point.

Perhaps the best advice of a general nature, before we get into specific technique, is this: don't ever hesitate to get help *ahead of time.* There is a very good reason why "The Playboy Advisor" is such a popular feature in *Playboy* magazine—not to mention the steady stream of books devoted to the subject of happiness in bed, and the enormous success of that ubiquitous lady doctor whose jolly wit has catapulted her from a "mere" advice columnist into a TV personality. The fact is, there is a lot of specialized knowledge about serious romance that we do *not* learn on our own, or at least not without making a lot of embarrassing mistakes first . . . and the same holds true with investing. No doubt, experience is a fantastic teacher, but learning *only* through experience can be frustrating, not to mention expensive. Before you learn the hard way, get a good head start by reading, talking with those more experienced than you (in this, as in love, believe no more than half the claims you hear!), and "doing it" in your head and on paper ahead of time.

OK, so you've done all your homework. Your immediate cash needs are well covered, you have reduced your debts to the point that you have excess money even *before* the next paycheck comes, and you have figured out how you are going to pay for the new roof your house needs this year. As part of your longer-term planning, you have decided to put some of your extra assets into common stocks. You are now ready to go.

Here, to help you on your way, are six of the finest bits of advice regarding "foreplay" we have ever seen, and they are equally valuable in your investing life *or* your social life. While there are never any guarantees in this life, these guidelines really work:

1. *Start slowly.* Rarely do opportunities come along that require truly instantaneous decisions and an immediate commitment of resources. If "the right moment" *does* pass, you can be sure it or another one just as attractive will come again. Looking for instant gratification seldom brings satisfactory results, and trying for a home run the first time at bat may cost you the game.
2. *Be patient.* A good approach takes time to bring results. "Warming up" is more than just a figure of speech, and getting there is half the fun anyway.
3. *Don't be afraid to experiment.* While it makes good sense to figure out what you do best and generally to stick with that technique, remember that different circumstances often require different approaches. The most successful technique is the one that gets you what you want.
4. *Stay on top.* The nature of everything in life is that it is in a constant state of change. Failure to stay on top of a situation leaves you extremely vulnerable as it evolves into something else. The best practitioners of any art stay completely in tune with the object of their attention.
5. *Push your luck* only *when things are going well.* The time to increase the stakes and go for a really big score is when everything is already going along beautifully, even better than you had planned. Conversely the *worst* time to push harder is when you sense greater resistance. On Wall Street, the real losers are those who consistently "average down," or

try to recoup a losing investment by pouring still more money into it, thus lowering their average cost per share but increasing their exposure to a losing investment. Probably the best adage for *all* aspects of life is "Cut your losses, and let your profits run."

6. *Know when to stop.* It makes a lot of sense, when you set out on an endeavor, to decide ahead of time what you can reasonably hope to achieve. Once you have succeeded to that degree, it makes even more sense to reconsider. Should you continue to try to get still more out of it? There is an optimal point at which to call it quits in every situation; unfortunately only with hindsight can we see that point clearly. For a more complete discussion of this topic, check out Chapter 10, "Going All the Way."

2
Know Your Partner Before You Bet Your Assets
(The Really Basic Stuff)

We read somewhere, a long time ago, a sociologist's suggestion that, prior to "tying the knot," all couples should be required to stand naked before each other in harsh lighting without any of the romantic trappings that accompany courtship. Following this "exposure" and a cooling-off period of a day or two, the couple would be permitted to marry if they still wanted to. The sociologist reasoned that both would have a realistic idea of just what they would be getting into. This, he concluded, would probably prevent some of the more disastrous liaisons made on the strength of perceived sex appeal and momentary passion.

If only, prior to the purchase of a stock, a close inspection of each investment were made thus! Just like the recommended "letting it all hang out" for the engaged couple, all investments should be stripped of their veneer, down to their basics. If value remains after inspection, then an investor can proceed in relative safety. The trick is to avoid swallowing some "cold call" pitch on a hot tip or investing on the basis of hunches, rumors, or brokerage house reports. Control your appetite (greed) with a healthy ratio of skepticism (fear).

Know your partner. Do some fundamental research and security analysis. Reams of books have been written on investing. As is typical, the professionals write for, and to, each other. It's like a roomful of computer programmers talking shop—satisfying to each other but unintelligible jibberish to the average person. It's typical overkill. The extent to which unnecessary security analysis is undertaken is legendary. You, the potential investor, can spend your entire adult life reading before exhausting the material and stepping into the investment arena yourself.

Investing doesn't have to be that way. Fundamental research is, in truth, quite simple. It focuses upon the financials and economics of the company. The necessary information is available as a result of disclosure requirements for publicly owned companies. All it takes is a little time and work to avoid being burned. But you must make the effort! Otherwise you are just gambling, and that doesn't work for long, whether it be in an investment relationship or a social one.

The individual investor need only stick to a few basics to enhance safety and performance. You will want to inspect four key areas: (1) financial strength, (2) profitability, (3) future prospects, and (4) relative value of the stock.

Your first step is to get the necessary data. The information is in shareholder annual and quarterly reports, press releases, and Securities and Exchange Commission (SEC) filings. All of this material can be obtained with a note or a phone call to the shareholder communications department at corporate headquarters.

Interim reports and press releases must be read. These will be quarterly financial results (often issued with a management message) and notice of dividend payments, stock splits, management changes, mergers, contract awards, and so on.

10Ks and 10Qs are very detailed annual and interim financial reports filed with the SEC. They can be quite revealing. The 8K must be filed following any material development. The 13D is an SEC filing required when any party, group, individual, or corporation reaches a 5 percent or greater ownership position in a publicly traded company. Such an event can mean anything from a straightforward investment position to the beginning of a takeover attempt. The filer must by law state the investor's intention. (It always helps to know who is in bed with you!) To receive these latter reports, you must request them from the company.

The most popular and best-known shareholder communication is the annual report. It may be very extensive or modest in size and scope but must, by law, contain vital data.

ONLY THE HAIR DRESSER KNOWS FOR SURE: GETTING A FEEL FOR THE COMPANY

Before getting into the financials, it is important to get a feel for the management culture and attitude. The annual report is the company's best foot forward. Management wants to make a good impression, and they will dress up the company in its Saturday-night best to seduce the shareholders. The letter to shareholders; the description of the company businesses, products, and/ or services; the rhetoric about the past year's performance and the company's prospects and direction—all provide insight into how management would like to be seen.

The mood of the annual report is very informative. If the year's progress and/or difficulties are intelligently reported, important insight into the management culture will be gained. On the other hand, be warned if the flavor is defensive and vague or if there is a preoccupation with the stock market and stock price. A partner who is always preening before the mirror is less likely to be an exciting and rewarding companion either for the evening or for the long pull. It is also sound policy to compare the latest shareholder letter to the prior year's. This will measure follow-through on management's expectations. It will give you a degree of, or lack of, confidence in management's current postulating.

Accompanying the annual report is the proxy. Read it in tandem with the annual report. It is somewhat of an exposé in that it spells out issues to be voted upon at the annual meeting and provides disclosures concerning directors, management, and transactions between the company and interested parties. Compensation packages of insiders are made public in the proxy. Too generous a compensation package is indicative of management abuse and disregard for shareholder interest. Also, the business before the shareholders at annual meetings will send any number of important signals. A new class of stock ("poison pills"), staggered terms for the board of directors, employee stock ownership plans (ESOPs), golden parachutes (generous exit compensation packages for senior executives), and an increase in the number of authorized common shares signal everything from management's entrenchment to a forthcoming financing project to stock splits and dividends. Some of these moves are in the best interest of the shareholder, while others are not.

LET'S GO NAKED:
THE FINANCIAL STATEMENTS

The bare facts are in the annual report. Every investor has the ability to analyze the financial statements. A few key standards, tests, and ratios will determine whether a company's position is favorable or unfavorable. Some may appear elementary, but they uncover the values important to recognize and pitfalls to avoid. By gaining a handle on the company's present financial position and operating record, the investor is better equipped to judge its future potential. And it is the future developments that ultimately determine the success of an investment.

You will find the following vital information in the annual report.

Financial Highlights

Normally located in a tabular format at the beginning of the annual report, financial highlights are the first step to financial intimacy. This element presents a two- to five-year history and comparison of selected financial data, such as total revenues, net income before taxes and extraordinary items, net income, total assets, working capital, shareholders' equity, net income per share, book value per share, cash dividend per share, and average number of shares outstanding.

The financial highlights provide your first factual insight into the company. The trend of the key measurements of the company's health, momentum, and aspirations is shown here. The financial highlights don't show all, but the section can certainly get you interested! As with the strippers at bachelor and bachelorette parties, the first few layers have been discarded. The more information shown, the more likely there is to be a revealing annual report.

If the company is in a sexy new industry, it may be

somewhat modest and unwilling to strut its financial wares prominently. These situations rank very low on the safety scale; the investor's capital is at greater risk. Such companies harbor the hope of becoming the next IBM and an enormous hit in the market but have no revenues, no earnings, no cash, and no assets. The biggest mistakes made by investors (the authors of this book included) are with stocks of companies "all on the come." Companies with a lot of promise but a poor record and no earnings are for a gambler, not a safety conscious investor. So, if the annual report's message promises much but delivers little, it's best to move on to safer opportunities.

And it is now time for you to move on to the "heavy breathing" of security analysis—the actual financial reports.

Checking for Potency of Earnings: Statement of Income (Profit and Loss)

Start with the profit and loss (P&L), a report of the past two years' operations that contains much greater detail than the aforementioned financial highlights. This will demonstrate if the company is growing and operating at an acceptable level of profitability. Anybody can act; but can they perform?

Revenues will be broken out by components such as services, product sales, licensing and consultant fees, investment profits, and interest and dividend income. Passive revenues such as interest, dividend, and investment revenues aren't valued as highly as sales and profits generated by operations. Wall Street tends to reward growth situations and discount passive revenue.

Cost of operations is also broken down, showing cost of goods sold, research and development costs, and selling, general, and administrative (SG&A) expenses. Here a few key financial ratios, gross profit and gross margin, are calculated.

Gross profit is the intermediate figure between gross revenue and net income. It is the money remaining after the cost of goods sold is deducted from total operating revenues, but before SG&A and other expenses are subtracted. The gross margin is the gross profit expressed as a percentage of total revenues. Only revenues from operations should be included in the calculation, not passive revenues. Management will often do the calculation for shareholders in the P&L, but it should be checked to verify that the calculation was based only on operating revenues.

The higher (wider) the gross margin, the better—the lower (narrower), the worse. Narrow gross margin, anything under 20 percent, can represent a host of difficult situations. An increase in cost of doing business could be devastating to net income (and to the price of the stock).

The following items should be scrutinized and measured as a percentage of sales.

Selling, General, and Administrative Expenses
SG&A data include officers' salaries, marketing costs, and all headquarters operating costs. Look for any significant changes from the prior year.

Income from Operations
Income from operations is the amount remaining after deducting the cost of goods sold, SG&A, and other expenses (except for interest expense) from total operating revenues. The operating margin is used to determine operating efficiency. Under 10 percent is considered too narrow in most industry groups.

Income Before Taxes
Tax rates vary. Some corporations are tax free or pay lower rates—reflecting tax shelters of one sort or another. To evaluate income between companies on as level a playing field as possible, compute income before

taxes as a percentage of revenues. Ideally, pretax margins should run a minimum of 15 percent.

Extraordinary Items

Items outside the experience of ordinary business, such as gains from the sale of an asset, write-offs, discontinued operations, severance costs, and loss due to fire or similar catastrophe, are extraordinary items. They can materially affect the P&L in a particular year. Each item must be considered separately, but extraordinary events should be factored out when analyzing the company's long-term outlook.

Net Income, Earnings per Share, and Price/Earnings Ratio

Net income is the amount remaining after all expenses, cost of doing business, and taxes are paid. The success of an investment depends upon its future earnings power. In formulating judgments of future expectations, investors are compelled to use current and past earnings as a guide. Study the P&L. It will provide insight into the trend and quality of earnings and give you the basis for an estimate of the future.

It is necessary to deal with earnings on a per share basis. The relationship between the company's earnings and the market price for the stock is expressed as a multiple of earnings. The price/earnings ratio (P/E) is the market price per share of stock divided by net income per share. For example, a $10 stock of a company earning $1 per share has a P/E of 10, or is said to be selling at ten times earnings. P/Es are calculated on either the latest annual earnings, latest twelve-month earnings, or estimated future earnings. Obviously it makes a difference which basis is used; when comparing P/Es of two or more companies, make sure you are using the *same*-basis P/E.

The P/E is a simple and valuable ratio by which stocks of companies in similar or different industries, of varying sizes, may be compared to one another and to the market in general. Market P/Es are easily located in *Barron's* "Market Laboratory" section, under the heading *Indexes, P/Es and Yields.* By comparing P/Es, you can determine if a stock is in or out of line. Also, Value Line (a premier investment service) lists composite statistics for P/Es of various industry groups. These are available in most public libraries.

The market assigns the lower P/E to the less popular stocks and the higher P/E to more attractive stocks. As a general rule, a low P/E is 8 or less, and a high P/E is 15-plus. It is wise to pass the high P/Es by. There is little sense and less safety in chasing the same stock that everyone else is running after. The majority is wrong the majority of the time; when the market ticks down (it always does!), these are the stocks that get slammed the hardest.

On the other hand, low-P/E stocks merit inspection. If the analysis of a stock holds up, an investment can be made even if the wizards of Wall Street have assigned a low P/E valuation. The low-P/E stock has a worst-case scenario already built into the price, and it is likely to weather a down market better. Besides, if the stock works out, the reward will be a double bang. That is, a higher P/E multiple on higher earnings. "Heads I win, tails I don't lose!"

As we stated earlier, preparing for the perfect date includes knowing as much as possible about your partner—both past history and present circumstances. The profit and loss (income) statement showed you the historic pattern of company operations. You also need to find out what the company looks like right now, at this point in time. Enter the balance sheet.

The Balance Sheet

The balance sheet functions as a "state of the union" report. Rather than a history of operations, the balance sheet is a still-life portrait. There are three major aspects to the balance sheet: assets, liabilities, and shareholder's equity.

Assets

Assets are composed of current, fixed, and some miscellaneous items. There are assets, and there are assets. Abundance of some is virtuous; others in quantity are unattractive and downright dangerous. A description of the primary assets follows.

Current Assets: *Cash and equivalents* (dollars and dollar items) are a current asset. Cash is king! A company must have enough to support operations, to meet obligations, and for a nest egg to weather the recessions and disruptions that occasionally plague businesses. Play it safe. Seek out companies with healthy cash levels. A 4 percent level of sales in cash is a minimum. The smaller the company, the larger the relative cash position should be. You don't want to court a partner who will put a cash squeeze on you!

Accounts receivable (what is owed the company over the near term) bear close watching. In real estate the three golden rules are location, location, and location. With regard to receivables, they are collection, collection, and collection. The quicker the collection, the better. It is a vital measure of a company. Otherwise the cash squeeze will become a crunch and the caress a stranglehold.

Receivables should not exceed 25 percent of total sales with a 2 percent allowance for doubtful accounts. More of either is a potential problem. Average collection periods run thirty to forty-five days. Up to sixty days is slow; over ninety days threatens to become uncollectible. Uncollectibility is usually acknowledged by the independent auditors with write-downs of accounts in arrears for over 120 days. In these instances the market unmercifully punishes the stock.

Inventories (raw material, work-in-process, and finished goods) are a third major category of current assets. Rising inventory levels can be a warning. Just as certain receivables may go bad, so may inventories become worthless due to obsolescence. Compare the percentage of inventory to sales with those of preceding years, using a like period in the fiscal year to allow for seasonality.

Inventory is measured by the number of times it turns in a year. To calculate turnover, divide the gross sales by the year-end inventory. The higher the turnover, the healthier the sales picture. Standards vary, but a turnover of 5 or more indicates a robust business.

The *remaining current assets* are usually not large and are worth little more than a glance. If an item is material, the explanation is in the financial footnotes. Be on the alert for capitalized and deferred expenses. These are expenses paid but not accounted for on the expectation that future operations will be there to apply against them. If future earnings don't appear, these deferred items will be expenses into the then-current P&L. Earnings can be hit hard, with disastrous consequences for the stock.

Fixed Assets: Fixed assets consist of buildings and improvements, fixtures, machines and equipment, tools, land and land improvements, and so on. Book value is reported in the annual report as the value of fixed assets net of their cost less accumulated depreciation (that portion of the assets' cost written off each year). For reporting purposes, with the exception of land holdings carried at cost, fixed assets decline in reported value each year. However, in the real world these assets may gain in value. Thus fixed assets may be understated, with actual present values in excess of those reported. In fact the true value is often well above that stated in the balance sheet. These are hidden assets and are obviously desirable.

Goodwill: Goodwill is an intangible asset—pure fluff. It is typically created when a company purchases an asset (or another company) at a price above its accounting value. Hence book value is overstated if intangibles are included. Intangibles eventually disappear as they are charged to income over the next forty years, thereby reducing reported income each year.

Miscellaneous Assets: Grouped together under other assets and placed at the very bottom of the asset side of the balance sheet, we find miscellaneous assets. They are usually insignificant.

Liabilities
The liability side of the balance sheet consists of current liabilities, long-term obligations, and reserves.

Current Liabilities: Current liabilities are debts and obligations payable within a year: trade accounts payable (money owed to vendors), accrued liabilities payable (bonuses and other small debts), income taxes accrued (unpaid portion of income taxes due), current maturities (portion of long-term obligations that must be paid within a year), and bank loans or notes payable (money borrowed from banks or others for the short term).

Long-Term Obligations: Long-term debt is as natural to companies as breathing is to you. Most firms have obligations that mature over many years, including bank loans and debt instruments such as bonds issued by the company. When the amount of long-term debt is too high relative to shareholder equity, then there is danger. The acceptable level of long-term debt is measured by a simple ratio of debt to capitalization, typically called "debt to equity ratio."

Reserves: Reserves are monies set aside to provide for future obligations and any potential liabilities. There are three basic categories of reserves: (1) liability reserves, which represent an obligation due at some future point, such as taxes, pending litigation, and customer refunds; (2) valuation reserves, which are offsets against the stated value of an asset (depreciation); and (3) surplus, or "voluntary," reserves, which hold part of reinvested earnings in reserve to provide for inventory write-downs. The footnotes to the financial statements will provide the details necessary to determine the true nature and importance of reserve accounts.

Shareholders' Equity

Shareholders' equity is the net worth of the company. It is the sum of two major ingredients, capital and earned surplus. The initial capital invested, by type of equity such as preferred stock and common stock, is classified as capital and/or capital surplus. Retained earnings, or earned surplus, are the sum total of all the company's net income and losses to the present. When divided by the number of shares issued and outstanding (that number is provided on the balance sheet), it equals book value per share. Book value theoretically is the value available for each share of common stock. It is a measurement with no practical value unless the company is actually being liquidated or sold, although the price of the company's stock is often compared to the book value per share.

Body Beautiful: Balance Sheet Financial Ratios

Bodybuilders flexing their biceps and beauty pageant contestants parading down the gangplank know full well the importance of having the right measurements. And they work to get those measurements. Without the right proportions they're just not contenders . . . and they won't get the opportunity to show the judges their other winning qualities.

Balance sheets are no different. Without a few vital measurements, they won't pass the first cut. A company must first have financial integrity to qualify for investor amour. A few more arrows in your quiver in addition to the ratios and valuations covered in the preceding section of the chapter, and the analytical repertoire is complete.

Here are a handful of easy-to-calculate key financial ratios and yardsticks. All may be computed quickly from the financial statements. In most instances they are already calculated and featured in the financial summary section of the annual report.

Current Ratio: The current ratio measures the ability to meet near-term debts as they come due. It is derived by dividing the total current assets by the total current liabilities. Current assets should exceed current liabilities by a wide margin, indicating that the company will have no difficulty in paying its bills. A current ratio of 2 to 1 is a standard minimum. That is, current assets should be at least twice the size of current liabilities. Anything less is trouble: a current ratio of 3 to 1 or better is preferable.

Acid Test, or Quick Test, Ratio: The acid test, or quick test, ratio is the ultimate test of a company's liquidity. Current liabilities are divided by the total of cash items plus receivables. It is customary to require that the cash items and receivables equal total current liabilities. Always apply the acid test!

Working Capital Ratio: Working capital is the capital

remaining after all near-term liabilities have been met. In other words it is the net of current assets less current liabilities. The ratio, expressed as the amount of sales per dollar of working capital, is calculated by dividing sales by working capital. For example, a company with $10 million in sales and $2 million in working capital would be said to have $5 in net sales per $1 in working capital.

The proper amount of working capital varies by the type of business. Companies enjoying a rapid turnover of inventory, such as food or apparel firms, will have high sales per dollar of working capital ($8-plus). Industrial companies, which must hold their inventories for long periods, have lower sales per dollar of working capital ($4 to $6). High-tech business requires the lowest ($3-plus).

The amount of working capital is *in*creased by net income, cash flow from depreciation and depletion, and injection of monies from sale of assets or stock. Rising inventories and receivables will also increase working capital. Working capital is *de*creased by investment in new equipment or plants and by dividend payments. A declining working capital signals that the business consumes capital faster than it can replace it. Generally speaking, changes in the working capital ratio require further investigation since they may result from positive *or* negative influences. For example, if a company is generating more sales per dollar of working capital, it may be due to greater productivity of its marketing effort. Conversely, the identical condition could mean a decline (an absolute decrease in working capital) as a result of an increase in current liabilities. Changes in financial position are normally carried as cash flow from operating activities or in a statement called source and application of funds.

Debt to Equity Ratio: The debt to equity ratio measures the degree of debt a company carries. It is calculated by dividing the total long-term debt outstanding
(on the right-hand side of the balance sheet ledger) by
the sum of that debt plus total shareholders' equity
(preferred stock, common stock, surplus, and reserves).
For example, if long-term debt is $25 million and share-
holders' equity is $62.5 million, you would divide $25
million by $87.5 million (the total of debt plus equity),
yielding 28.5 percent. Hence debt represents 28.5 percent of the company's total invested capital. Debt up to
40 percent is OK; more than that requires some cau-
tion. At 60 percent there is just too much leverage for
the sensible investor.

Statements of Changes in Financial Position, Retained Earnings, and Shareholders' Equity

As their names indicate, these statements provide an
accounting of changes in the respective areas for the
fiscal year. An investor can follow the source and use of
cash, item by item. Each statement concludes with a
net increase or decrease in the position being tracked.

This section of the annual report is must reading,
particularly in tandem with the financial ratios and
measurements discussed. Positive cash flow from operations is desirable. It means a company can finance its
growth strictly from operations, without the need of
costly outside financing. Negative cash flow indicates
the company will require outside help at some point in
the future.

Management's Discussion and Analysis of Financial Condition and Results of Operations

The annual report's "true confessions" section is required by law. Unlike the letter to shareholders, this segment of the annual report compares four years of operating results, with frequent reference to percentage and dollar changes and the reasons underlying them. Combined with the study of the financial statements, this can be particularly informative.

Notes to Financial Statements

Explanatory notes will clear up most confusion in the financial statements. At the very least, the notes should be scanned.

ANNUAL REPORT OF INDEPENDENT ACCOUNTANTS

The auditor's letter, or statement, is short and usually "boilerplate." On occasions when there is a problem, the independent accountants will issue a "qualified opinion" questioning the firm's practices or even its ability to continue in business. Certainly this is something every safety-minded investor should be cognizant of.

TO KNOW THEM IS TO LOVE THEM?

Earning power is the major determining factor in a stock's price, and ultimately more weight should be assigned to it—but not to the exclusion of the other considerations covered here. A study of *all* the data is necessary to reach an informed opinion on a stock's merit. With some work and discipline it is possible to outperform the market and the so-called professional experts. Knowing your partner (the company whose stock you may buy) is the first and biggest step toward that objective. So get to know your partner *before* you bet your assets.

3
Playing the Field
(Why Monogamy Is Such a Bad Idea on Wall Street)

Right off the bat, let's get one thing straight: we are 100 percent in favor of annual family picnics; low fixed-rate mortgages; lifetime marriages based upon love, compassion, and mutual appreciation; and the American Way in general. Having said that, however, we must admit noticing one apparent contradiction in the way we mere mortals are wired together. The passion that undergirds our ambition to achieve the above-mentioned goals, whether material or matrimonial, is the self-same one that at times threatens to get us in the most trouble. We yearn for the stability of uncomplicated long-term relationships with a single focus; but, at the same time, we find such relationships so attractive that we may want to have several of them—maybe even several at the same time!

MONOGAMY VERSUS HUMAN NATURE

It is desirable and perhaps even necessary to pass through a number of preliminary relationships in order to learn the ropes, develop the skills, and identify the best candidate—the one with whom we ultimately expect to settle down. Once that target has been selected, however, we are expected to undergo a complete and instantaneous metamorphosis, shedding any vestige of interest in anything or anyone other than the object of our desire. Once you have tried the Jaguar, the Porsche, and the Miata, and then you buy the BMW, you are expected to lose every shred of interest in the other cars. The same thing is true, doubled and redoubled in spades, when it comes to our more intimate social relationships.

The quirk of human nature that works against these expectations has been addressed by different cultures in different ways throughout human history—and resolved with varying degrees of success. In twentieth-century America we tend to pretend the problem doesn't really even exist. We treat deviations from our puritanical tradition of hard work and single-minded devotion as temporary lapses, to be neither noticed nor remarked upon unless absolutely necessary. The guilt that can result from such a hidden fall from grace is the stuff of which entire careers in counseling and self-help authorship are made.

Well, there *is* hope. Not only are the flower children still alive and well in the world, they have become extremely successful by applying their free-love approach to investment strategy. As it turns out, Wall Street not only is more tolerant of such shenanigans than is Main Street, it positively demands that the successful investor *not* be married to any given investment for better or for worse, forsaking all others, no matter what!

Actually, two distinct points need to be made here. First, there are no such things as "one-decision" stocks which you can buy and then put away forever and ever.

Times change, technologies change, companies change, and *you* change, both in terms of your needs and the extent of your risk tolerance. While some stocks may turn out to be faithful soul mates for years and years, such a blissful state can never be taken for granted. There is an appropriate time to sell *every* stock; when you read Chapter 10 you will learn all about it.

Second, in investing (unlike the rest of life) you do not want to focus—in fact you do not *dare* to focus—all your love and affection upon a single recipient. The risk of failure *and even more so the penalties for failure* are just too great. While statistics are saddening, the truth is that a great many marriages are doomed to fail. Despite the emotional trauma of the ensuing divorce, however, most individuals not only survive but then move on in search of happier circumstances. In investing, if you put all your chips into a single investment and it goes sour, you can be up to your neck in some pretty foul stuff. Thus we approach the subject of diversification.

Simply stated, diversification means reducing the risks that are inherent in every investment vehicle by putting your money into a number of different examples (of stocks, for instance) across a variety of distinct industry groups: spreading your largess around, as it were, and limiting your exposure to any single stock, industry group, or type of investment. In other words, play the field.

Few would argue that diversification is not a good thing. There is some question, however, as to exactly how much diversification you need to achieve the maximum insurance against an unexpected development that could otherwise devastate your entire investment program. At one end of the spectrum is the position held by one eminent market guru. He refers to certain academic studies that demonstrate that you can achieve almost 90 percent of the entire benefits of diversification by holding just eight different stocks, so long as these are taken from several different industry groups. He also suggests that, depending upon the size of the overall portfolio, the appropriate level of diversification can range from four to five stocks (in a portfolio with a total value of $20,000) to as many as twenty or more stocks in a portfolio with a combined value of $250,000 or greater. Another well-known stock market writer cites his need to stay in touch with all developments affecting the companies in which he invests. Thus he feels that ten to twenty stocks are the most he can effectively handle in a portfolio while still achieving sufficient diversification, no matter how big the portfolio in terms of its absolute value.

For the investor with a relatively small amount of capital to put to work in the stock market, diversification presents a special problem. Dividing, say, $25,000 into ten different issues of approximately equal size could be justified on the grounds that the investor wished to achieve sufficient diversification. Ten investments of roughly $2,500 each would, however, involve rather substantial brokerage commissions, arising from the small size of each position and the possible need for an odd-lot differential in several cases.

In such a situation you might well consider the use of a mutual fund rather than constructing your own portfolio. In addition to furnishing the presumed benefits of full-time professional portfolio management, mutual funds provide risk protection via diversification that goes well beyond virtually every definition of what is needed. The funds often hold dozens of different stocks within each of many different industry groups. The best-known example of this is the multibillion-dollar Magellan Fund, which holds literally hundreds of companies' shares at any time. The goal in this case was not simply diversification: it reflected the fund manager's unusual (and exceedingly successful) personal investment style.

In the 1950s the concept of a "fund of funds" was wildly successful, largely on the marketing platform that such an investment reduced the underlying risk even further by diversifying across several different investment managers as well as across industry groups and individual stocks. A potential problem, of course, was that all these funds really may have accomplished was to cancel out the effect of each individual fund manager's intelligence, skill, and judgment. They created a hybrid blend of the same basic stocks, representing *nobody's* best guess as to the proper weighting to be given in the overall portfolio. There has been a resurgence of this concept in recent years, with a proliferation of investment advisors and market letter writers whose professed expertise lies in their ability to recommend an "ideal" package of mutual funds to individual investors. Given the need to pay management fees, administration expenses, and in some cases "loads" or other marketing charges to each of the individual funds, the additional cost of such advice and the possibility of diluting the investment strategy of each fund make the potential for incremental gains from this approach questionable.

Appropriate diversification plays a valid and necessary role in the management of risk in your investment portfolio. It makes being an overall winner possible without your having to be a genius at picking the single stock that doubles or triples regardless of general economic conditions (invariably when it is in somebody else's portfolio!). It also will keep you from becoming the victim of a totally unanticipated development affecting your company's fortunes.

In short the concept of diversification requires that—no matter how decent you may be otherwise—to be a successful investor you should think and act like a real playboy in your relationships with the stocks you own. In the best sense, you should become totally wrapped up in them, obsessed with knowing all about them, playing the strengths of one against the weaknesses of another so as to satisfy your every investment idea or desire. But remember, you can't really trust them to stay the wonderful way they were (or you *thought* they were) when you first committed to them. You must be ready to love 'em and leave 'em. And if you want to be sure of getting the "right date to the prom," you had better have an entire black book of possibilities working at any one time. That way, at the end of the day, you will be able to go back to the spouse, the kids, the dog, and the house in the suburbs true blue and faithful, content with your life and with a successful investment strategy that leaves you the envy of your friends.

4
Never, Ever Go
Without Protection!
(How to Avoid Nasty and Unwanted Side Effects)

Whether or not your mother or father ever actually took you aside (amid great hmming and aahing) to tell you officially what you had inevitably already learned as part of the oral tradition conferred on you in the upper reaches of elementary school, one of the biggest deals in the facts of life discussion was the part about protection.

Generally, the objective of protection was never really spelled out. Rather the obliqueness of the references and the overwhelming vagueness of the discussion ensured that, if you didn't already know what on earth your parent was talking about, you certainly couldn't divine it from what was being said. Well, thanks to the elevated levels of social consciousness and the commendable progress toward direct communication that have arisen from the much-touted sexual revolution, the truth can now be told straight out. Dear old Mom or Dad was trying to save your young self, not just from sexual misadventure but from financial distress as well.

Protection—the means to guard against any unanticipated, painful, and unhealthy consequences while
maintaining the highest degree of comfort, satisfaction,
and overall pleasure—is obviously much to be desired
in the area of romance. This is just as true when you put
your *money* into something tempting!

Five basic kinds of protection should be fully understood by every individual investor. One or more of
these will be appropriate at any given time in the stock
market. (Actually, there are others as well, but most are
simply adaptations of the basic five.) Three of these
methods of protection are suited for both bull and bear
markets, and two of them are most appropriate when
the element of market risk is deemed to be especially
high. In investing, just as in sex, there is no such thing
as 100 percent protection (short of total abstinence,
heaven forbid!). But using one or more of these techniques will vastly improve your odds of avoiding investment catastrophes, while greatly improving your peace
of mind and thus your enjoyment—which is, after all,
the point.

1. STOP-LOSS ORDERS:
THE ORIGINAL "SAFES"

Every time you purchase a stock, without exception,
enter a stop-loss order to sell it. A stop-loss order is a
sell order that will automatically be executed if and
when the price of the purchased stock falls to the level
specified in the stop-loss. *Where* to set the stop-loss is
the hard part and has been the subject of entire chap-
ters of books on investing. Unless you have the time
and the inclination to develop the ideal stop-loss price
for each stock, reflecting its historical volatility and
chart behavior, you are probably better off using a
simple rule of thumb that reflects your own comfort

level. A commonly used rule of 10–15 percent below purchase price normally will make sense. Obviously, a 10 percent stop-loss will take you out of more positions than will a 15 percent one but with less damage before the stop-loss is triggered.

Most of us probably remember the macho dude stories about not wanting to use protection because it is "like wearing a raincoat in the shower." It is an absolute certainty that sooner or later you will inevitably buy a stock that promptly sinks to your stop-loss point, triggers the sale (at a loss for you), then turns around and does what you bought it for in the first place—it takes off like a rocket. When that happens, you will hate yourself. You will hate the authors of this book even more. However, this rare occurrence is an extremely small price to pay for the protection a stop-loss order affords against unforeseen developments in either the overall economy or in the outlook for the particular company.

Not only can a stop-loss order minimize a sudden turn against your position, it can protect against an even more insidious, gradual deterioration in price. In the latter case, human nature being human nature, the investor finds it exceedingly difficult to keep from hanging on "just a little bit longer," thus transforming a modest loss into a major one. On Wall Street, as in love, sticking with a bad relationship in the hopes that it will turn itself around has a 99 percent guarantee of failure.

The basic logic behind the routine use of stop-loss orders is irrefutable. When you buy a stock, you buy it because your understanding of the company's business prospects, in the context of the current and anticipated economic environment, tells you that the stock price is lower than it should be, and lower than it *will* be when other potential buyers of the stock appreciate its value in the same way that you do. You hope either that others will discover its potential as you have or that, over time, your predictions about the company's prospects will in fact turn out to be true. You certainly do *not* buy the company's stock in the anticipation that it will go down! Thus a decline in the price of your stock can only mean that, for whatever reason, the thinking behind your decision to purchase the stock at the price you paid is not in sync with whatever is actually driving the price of the stock. In other words, no matter how good your reasons might have been, whatever turned you on is not turning the stock on in the same way—and that is one dangerous and unhappy situation to be in. Remember, the market does not have to accept your reasons for buying a stock, no matter how right you "should" have been.

In the blissful event that your newly purchased stock does indeed go up in price, the stop-loss order fulfills another valuable function; it will lock in the profits your wisdom and canny foresight have so justly earned you, and it can help you decide when to sell the stock. Selling a stock at the right time is probably even more difficult than buying it, because a stock's price will frequently reach a peak *before* all the good things about the company have actually come true. Frequent readjustment of your stop-loss order, bringing it up under the price of the stock as that price moves higher, will allow the market itself to tell you when enough is enough.

2. INDEX PUTS AND CALLS

Put and call options (which convey the right—but not the obligation—to sell or to buy at a predetermined price), whether on stocks or on stock market indices such as the Major Market Index (XMI) or the S&P 100 (OEX), serve two legitimate but quite different purposes. First, they can be used by speculators to place short-term, highly leveraged bets on the direction of an individual stock or of the overall market. The risk of loss is great, but the potential reward can be enormous if the speculator is right, and is right immediately. Speculating with options is very racy stuff. It is great fun if you are winning, but you can bleed to death before you even know you have been cut. The jaded would-be speculator should look into such titillating option strategies as "spreads," "straddles," and "ratio backspreads;" for the truly kinky, there are "long condors," "butterflies," and even "short strangles"! Though not quite as hairy as commodity trading, speculating in options has no legitimate place in the investment strategy for most of us.

The other purpose, the one most investors absolutely *should* know about, is that of hedging a portfolio of stocks against an overall market decline in which—like the police raid on the brothel—they take away the good ladies along with the bad ones.

The purchase of an index put option as a means of protection is in concept exactly like the purchase of an insurance policy. It covers a specific period of time, it provides for payment to the holder in the event of specific levels of disasters, and you hope like hell that you never need to make a claim on it! This latter point is most important, because it is sometimes easy to conclude, having hedged a portfolio a few times against disasters that do *not* occur, that you really don't need the insurance after all and that the money was therefore wasted. For some reason, we seem to understand the cost-of-protection concept more easily when we are talking about life insurance. (Have you ever met anyone who *wanted* to collect on his or her own life insurance?)

The point is, for a relatively modest sum, index put options can be purchased that will appreciate in value if the underlying index *de*preciates, but will normally expire with no value at all if the market as reflected in the underlying index does not go down. The amount of protection and the extent to which even a modest decline (or a stable market) can be hedged against are variables that can be addressed by using options with different strike prices relative to the current index value. In times when the risks in the marketplace are particularly high, the use of index put options as hedges can provide excellent protection while allowing you to continue to participate actively in the stock market.

Your broker should be able to explain in complete detail the use of index options as hedges and to recommend specific strikes and specific maturities to you. A complete guide to option strategies can also be obtained free of charge by writing to the Chicago Board Options Exchange (CBOE), LaSalle at Van Buren, Chicago, IL 60605. Excellent option-related material can also be obtained without charge by writing to the New York Stock Exchange, Inc., 20 Broad Street, New York, NY 10005.

3. WRITING COVERED CALLS

Sometimes what is covered up is even more exciting and enticing than what is fully exposed. When you think the market has only limited potential for gain in the near term or that there is considerable risk that the market may even go down but you do not want to liquidate individual stocks you already hold, you should consider the strategy of writing (selling) calls against the stocks you want to keep. This very conservative strategy involves giving up the right to any *substantial* appreciation in the stock's price over a specified time period. In return you gain a dollar premium that effectively cushions the stock price against any downturn during the same time frame, and you generate additional income beyond the dividend in the event that the stock price remains stable.

By writing covered calls (calls against stocks you already own), your entire risk is that you will have to sell the stocks you have specified, at the price you have specified, at some point during the limited time period covered by the option. It is not entirely foolproof; there is always the possibility of a takeover offer or some other unexpected and dramatic good news that may cause a big rise in the stock. If you have written calls on those stocks, you will be forced to sell them at the strike price of your calls, and you will benefit from the rise only to the extent that the calls you wrote were "out of the money" (at a higher strike price than the current price of the stock) when you wrote them. Since you presumably are relatively bullish on the stock's outlook (otherwise why wouldn't you have sold this stock if you also thought the market looked weak?), it would probably be a good idea to sell calls at a strike price that would represent at least a modest increase over the current price. That way you are still allowing for some gain to occur, and you will be able to keep the entire premium received from selling the call. The best outcome in this case would be for the price of the stock to rise to a point just *below* the strike price at the expiration of the call, leaving the call worthless, the stock price higher, and the premium firmly in your pocket. Actually history has demonstrated that the majority of calls so written do in fact expire worthless, since the best indicator of the future price of a stock, at any point in time, turns out to be its present price.

4. WRITING NAKED PUTS

Under very special circumstances, this slightly obscene-sounding strategy can provide an excellent way to increase your protection against the unanticipated and unpleasant side effects that can befall even the most careful denizen of Wall Street.

The Fall of 1990 appears to have been one of those times. With virtually all measures of the stock market signaling that we were in a true bear market, and may have been in one for much of the previous year, the fortunate investor had utilized stop-loss orders and perhaps had added to available cash through the use of index puts and covered calls. He or she was then positioned to begin to look for investment vehicles to utilize when the market finally hit bottom, and a new bull market cycle began again. Bottom-fishing, or trying to time the exact bear-market low, is an exceedingly hazardous occupation, because stocks that appear to be unreasonably cheap can and often will become unreasonably even cheaper! At some point, however, the bargains become truly compelling, and the long-term investor will have developed a short list of candidates that scream out to be bought even if, in the short run, their prices happen to deteriorate a little more. In such a situation, writing naked (i.e., uncovered) puts on stocks you *want* to own, at a price you would be willing to pay, is definitely worthy of consideration.

Here is an example of just how this can work. In late September 1990 the stock of Schering-Plough (SGP) corporation was trading in the low forties. An investor, having watched this high-quality stock come down from a twelve-month high of 50¾ only weeks before, might decide to buy four hundred shares if the price went to 40, regardless of the overall market's vulnerability. At that point, with the price of SGP at 43½, the investor could have written four puts on SGP, with a strike price of 40, expiring in late October, for a premium (price) of 1½. In so doing, the investor would accomplish two things. First, if the price of SGP *did* drop to 40 or below, the puts would presumably be exercised, and the investor would then be required to pay $40 per share for the SGP shares—a decision already reached in any case—but the price actually paid would be only 38½ (not counting commissions) due to the offsetting effect of the options sold. Second, if the price of the Schering stock did *not* go to the buy point of 40, the option would expire worthless and the proceeds of the four puts—some $600 before commissions—would be the investor's to keep. As added protection when bottom-fishing, this is definitely a technique to consider but should only be used for stocks you are sure you want to own.

5. SHORT SELLING

Most active investors are invested virtually all the time. Studies have shown, however, that the market is headed higher only about 65 percent of the time, and is headed lower about 35 percent of the time. In other words, you are fighting the odds about one-third of the time. At best, investors will withdraw from the game altogether when they sense that they are in a bear market. Yet a simple strategy can let you take advantage of the major market direction close to 100 percent of the time! Even when you are not sure about the market's major thrust, that technique—selling short—can allow you to hedge at least part of your investment against losses due simply to market direction. Hey, you are going to score more often if you go with the flow!

In concept, short selling is simplicity itself. In a normal, or "long," situation you look for stocks you think will go up. In a bull market your stock picks will be further buoyed by the overall market direction. Even in a bear market your choices will hopefully go down less than other, less-deserving stocks. As a short seller, on the other hand, you look for companies whose stock you believe will do poorly, no matter what the overall direction of the market. In a bear market, these stocks should really get creamed. Such stocks are sold short (actually they are borrowed through your broker and then sold), with the intent of buying them back (covering) at some future time at a lower price. The objective, as always, is to buy low and sell high; in a short sale only the timing is reversed.

There are two reasons why selling short is so rarely undertaken by the individual investor. In the first place, betting on a company's poor performance is considered un-American. This is, of course, pure hogwash. The price of a company's stock will go up or down according to the market's perception of the value of the company and its prospects, regardless of whether you have bought it or sold it. It is no less honorable for you to sell General Motors short, for example, than it is for you to sell GM stock you happen to own, if you think the outlook for the stock is poor. Selling a company's stock short does not put extra pressure on the stock's price; on the contrary, since it must eventually be covered it represents potential buying pressure.

The second reason why most nonprofessionals are afraid to short a stock is the old bugaboo that in theory the potential loss in a short sale is unlimited. If you short a stock, there is potentially no end to the damage you can suffer, since the price can theoretically keep on rising indefinitely against you. The safeguard against such a hypothetical disaster, of course, is that whenever you sell short you always enter a protective stop-loss buy order at a price 10–15 percent above your short sale. This automatically covers your position (and your derrière at the same time) should your bet against a particular stock turn sour.

You should also be aware of the "uptick rule," which requires that a short sale of a listed stock must always be made at a higher price than the previous transaction. In other words, a short sale cannot be executed when the price is declining. The aim of this rule is to preclude the theoretical possibility that massive short selling by itself could otherwise drive down the price of a stock.

Dear old Mom and good old Dad had lots of good advice. They probably also said, at one time or another, that there is a time and a place for everything. Protection against disaster in your investing is *always* appropriate, and these five techniques are the basic ones that every lover of Wall Street should consistently practice, no matter how hot and heavy the action gets.

5
Casual $ex
(The Ins and Outs of Day Trading)

We live in the fastest-moving society in history. Of all the areas of our existence—communication, travel, manufacturing, services, individual mobility, wealth, consumption of goods, health care, education, and technological advances—only transportation seems to be slowing down as it is replaced with faster and faster means of transmitting and processing information. Just as the productive elements of our lives have sped up, so has the social environment. Today everything is done with dispatch. Acting with deliberation does not merit the accolade it used to, nor is it likely ever to do so again.

As a logical extension of this acceleration, our society has become preoccupied with instant gratification. Personal freedom and recreation have become central to living in most walks of life.

We are on the fast track to stay. You don't believe it? Look around. Everywhere we see fax machines, instant lotteries, microwave food, one-hour photo processing, round-the-clock bank access for shoppers and depositors, mobile phones, mobile everything, and—heaven help us—maybe soon a twenty-four hour a day, seven days a week stock market!

Nowhere is the desire for instant gratification more evident than in the financial markets. Day traders thrive in this environment. Like the social butterfly who moves rapidly from one engagement to another without entanglements, the day trader buys and sells stocks and/or options daily, with price objectives measured in minutes and hours. To the day trader, stocks are merely numbers, and the longer-term business prospects for the companies themselves are not just unimportant, they are totally irrelevant.

ARE YOU A FLIRT OR A LOVER, A GAMBLER OR AN INVESTOR?

An entire culture has been established to accommodate the fast pace of today's stock markets. As if stock trading weren't enough, a universe of derivative speculative devices has been created to put more spin on the market as well. We are not going to recommend them. The average investor doesn't have the facilities (access to trading floor–level computer terminals, very sophisticated software, etc.) or the funds or the total dedication of effort needed to utilize these devices effectively. Also they can be exceedingly dangerous to your financial health. You can get your head handed to you in moments! Further, the most successful techniques are very complex and typically used by sophisticated institutional and very large individual investors to hedge their portfolios or to undertake arbitrage. Remember, the purpose in a casual situation, either social or business, is to keep it simple and loose. If it gets complicated, it ain't casual anymore. A person having a casual affair doesn't want to get involved. Involved isn't what day trading is about, either.

We also do not recommend speculating in futures, where you can bet on underlying commodities such as currencies, government bonds, metals, and soybeans. By playing these futures and the options on them, the investor is betting on future moves, up or down, of the market for a commodity or of the stocks within a specific industry group.

You need a broad-based move to make trades in these indices pay off. Also these are not one- or two-day affairs: they can last for weeks or even months. (They do, however, serve a purpose in that they can correctly telegraph the market's mood in the immediate and intermediate term, and this is critical to the day trader.)

The speculator is not *investing* in anything, even for the briefest moment. Rather he's betting on the roll of the dice at the crap table or gambling on which raindrop moving on a window pane will reach the sill first. We regard these vehicles as more appropriate for the casino than the stock market. We are aggressive investors, not gamblers. Not that there is anything wrong with gambling—it just should not be confused with investing.

BETTING ON THE SPREAD

The present can be judged against future expectations by looking at the market for index futures contracts. It's quite simple. Let's say the Standard & Poor's (S&P) 500 stock index is trading at 308.50 at present. This is called the "cash" index since it is an absolute—it is the real-time value of the moment. Now let's take the index futures. Assume the futures contract that expires three months down the road is selling at 315.17. That is the

level at which the crapshooters (Oops, excuse us! Investors?) are betting the market will be at that time, as
measured by the S&P 500. The difference between the
cash level and the futures is the spread. The larger the
spread, the more bullish the immediate market outlook.
The narrower the spread, the less bullish the outlook.
And if the future is at a discount to the cash (that is, the
value of the futures contract is less than the value of the
cash index), the outlook is quite bearish. The farther
out the index futures expires, the greater the spread is
likely to be. This is because the premium demanded by
the seller of the futures contract is greater, since he or
she has extended the contract over a longer period. As
a rule, the futures contract expiring within three
months is the most often traded.

Rather than getting bogged down in detail, remember that it's the trend of the spread, premium or
discount, that is important to the day trader. Since
these spreads are established with real money (speculators set them with hard dollar investments), they have a
certain validity as stock market barometers. In fact,
spreads are not very different from the odds at a race-
track, which are set by the consensus of bets on the
horses running. Spreads are constantly changed by
speculators placing their bets, and they can be called
up on a Quotron at any moment, just like the price of a
stock.

THE SELF-FULFILLING PROPHECY: PROGRAM TRADING

As if it were not enough to devise these contrived
trading vehicles, enter now the self-fulfilling prophecy:
program trading. Program trading is a computerized
trading technique. It emerged as a tool for major institutional investors to lessen investment risks in their

portfolios. Program trading has been part of the Wall Street scene since the early 1980s. But not until the postmortem of the 1987 crash and the 1989 minicrash was the impact of these programs fully appreciated.

Program trading triggers the simultaneous buying or selling of hundreds of stocks. Briefly it works like this: When the spread between cash values and futures values of the index being traded reach certain predetermined levels, the computer kicks in and trades tons of stocks. It offsets the trade by simultaneously purchasing or selling an equivalent position in the index futures contracts. Then, when the spread returns to a more normal relationship, the program trades will be "unwound" by doing the exact opposite of what has been done before, allowing the program trader to make a small but significant profit on a risk-free basis.

There are services that follow program trading and have a pretty good feel, moment to moment, as to what will trigger a computer buy or sell program. A broker who is any good should have access to these services. When activated, such programs can almost immediately drive prices up or down, creating enormous and volatile swings in market prices, often precipitating buying or selling panics.

THE GAME IS AFOOT! WHEN TO PLAY AND WHEN TO KEEP HANDS OFF

The cash-to-futures relationship as a daily market indicator used in concert with an understanding of program trading is the day trader's best friend. Aside from the obvious, being on the correct side (buy or sell) of the market, there are key considerations.

First, are you set up emotionally to handle the pace (and stress) of day trading? Only you know if you're made that way. Are you a kiss 'em and forget 'em

person? Are you able to make decisions and act
quickly? Do you have the commitment to the trading
mystique that at times requires the equivalent of ice
water in your veins? Can you hit and run, be it with
profit or loss? Or are you the studious type who will
worry a situation to death? If your answer is yes to all
the questions except the last, then read on. If not, well,
the exercise did you good anyway. An understanding of
index futures, arbitrage, and program trading can only
help you cope with today's financial markets.

Second, is it a good trading market? Examine both
the market indices and the major stocks. It's as much a
market of stocks as it is a stock market. Here's what to
look for:

1. *Volatility.* Do you see abrupt advances and declines
   in stock prices, particularly shares of mainstay companies? Look for daily full-point and larger moves in
   a broad spectrum of stocks and industry groups.
   You're looking for major moves across the board,
   either up or down, in these bellwether issues. In the
   best trading market such stocks seesaw all day, exac-
   erbating volatility and enhancing opportunities for
   the trader.
2. *Liquidity.* What today might be considered light
   volume would have boggled the mind in the sixties
   and seventies. It is not enough for a stock to trade in
   wide swings. You also want to see market liquidity.
   The stock targeted should trade heavily. A high average daily volume of shares changing hands will provide the day trader the opportunities to buy and sell
   in adequate volume without disrupting the market
   for the stock.

The *Wall Street Journal, Investor's Daily,* and

Barron's will provide information about volatility and liquidity. Today's stock market has all the necessary elements to enable someone to day-trade profitably. There is money to be made for those willing to commit to "one-day stands." Day traders generally like to be "flat" when the market closes business for the day. That is, they don't hold any positions—not even overnight, if they can avoid it, and never over the weekend or holiday. Remember, these are casual relationships; you don't want to have coffee with them in the morning!

RULES TO TRADE BY

You might remember your parents referring to local craftspeople practicing their skills as knowing their "stock in trade." Certainly your parents were not referring to the stock market, but never was a phrase more apropos than that one is for casual stock ownership. The question is how to practice the art safely and profitably. Here are six simple guidelines:

1. *Be adequately financed.* Have a pool of capital set aside dedicated to day trading. In this game, you have to commit a decent amount. A minimum would be $25,000. The trader is looking to scalp fractions of a point in profits. A home run is a point or more of profit made. The size of the position must be meaningful to make this all worthwhile. Of course, the stake can be increased materially by buying on margin, but this is not something we would recommend in most markets. It certainly isn't safe!
2. *Whenever possible, trade daily with stocks that may be held beyond the day if necessary.* The quality of the stock should have long-term staying power. Do not select thinly traded or second- and third-tier stocks.

3. *Negotiate commission rate as low as possible.*
Since you're trading in fractions of a point of profit,
literally every penny in commissions paid per share
is meaningful. The maximum amount a successful
day trader can afford is around 10 cents a share. If
you play your cards right and you represent a decent
account to your broker, the rate can be quite low—
4 to 6 cents a share if trading frequently enough.
Thus, it is possible to trade within fractions of a
point and still turn a tidy profit.

4. *Set trading goals and stick to them.* Don't get
greedy. Cut losses. Simple advice but rarely followed
by the individual investor. If your study of a stock
shows a daily one-point trading range, take the ½
point or so profit and run. Your goal is to make a
little money each trade, trading as often as possible.
If the stock moves away from you by ½ point or so,
take your loss quickly and move on to the next
trade. The first loss is always the smallest!

5. *Be in constant touch with the market and with
your trading positions.* In the "old days" brokerage
firms had boardrooms where the tape, reporting
every trade on the exchanges, ran across a highly
visible display. Customers, traders, and "walk-ins"
would sit before the display and read the tape as it
ran across the screen. Today that is archaic. The
tape and the market action are just too fast. You
must either (1) have a dedicated broker who will
monitor the positions for you and execute orders
accordingly, (2) utilize a computer terminal where
you can program in your trading positions and enter
your orders directly, or (3) use stop orders to take
profits or cut losses (see Chapter 4). Since we doubt
that the average investor's portfolio is large enough
to command the necessary attention of a single
broker, the latter two are the only real options.

6. *Learn to read charts*. You don't have to be an expert, but you *do* have to be able to understand support levels, resistance, gaps, and so on. There are many, many textbooks on charting and technical analysis; both your local librarian and your broker should be able to point you in the right direction. Virtually every financial newspaper covers the subject, and there are subscription services available as well. If you're gonna trade, you're gonna have to track the price movements!

There is money to be made trading stocks in today's volatile markets. However, it takes work. Practice on paper first. Pick and track daily a selection of qualified stocks; trade them mentally as you would with real money. Then, when you get a feel for it, make your move into the arena of day trading.

6
Bull Markets and Bare Knees
(The Hemline Index of Stock Prices)

Any experienced investor, or for that matter anyone with even the most fleeting experience with the stock market, will tell you the market is ruled by passion. All the rationalizations in the world cannot dispel this truism.

How many times have you heard someone describe a date as "He's such a nice guy" or "She has a swell personality." Yeah sure (big yawn)! No one is gonna break down any doors on that one. But what about "He's hot" or "Check it out"? That's when you're cooking. That's when you're motivated. That's action. And action is what the stock market is all about. It is a double-edged sword. It is a roller coaster. It can carry a stock or a market trend to the heights of riches, or it may utterly crater a stock in a headlong reckless crash.

We equate passion with sex. Sex, the relationship and attitudes existing between the genders, is volatile. It has highs and lows. Attitudes between men and women fluctuate from warm to cool to cold to white hot.

We, being a civilized society (hah!), dress according to the moment—in our economic state as well as in our romantic mood. You have only to take a walkabout, as they say in Australia, and observe the dress code and behavior of the people during a recession or a boom. In boom years your eyes will become unglued; the "scenery" is soooo beautiful! On the other hand, you will become absolutely despondent at the gray "landscape" that parades by during hard times, recession, unemployment, and a bear market.

To the same extremes that members of the opposite sex go in their views of each other—adore or abhor, wild abandon or restraint—so goes stock market sentiment. How to measure the "vibes" of the moment? Well, women's fashions are a proven and most visible barometer. Therein lies the foundation of the theory for the hemline index of stock prices. That and, of course, the historical correlation of the behavior of hemlines and stock prices.

DO SKIRTS AND STOCK PRICES GO UP AND DOWN TOGETHER? THE HEMLINE THEORY

Believe it or not, there actually exists a long-term relationship between fashion and money. *Fashion*, by the way, is a generic word. In addition to its traditional application to jeans, swimsuits, skirts, men's pleated trousers, or plus fours, fashion is part of many facets of life: pop, country and western, rock and roll, blues, or soul music; bungee cord jumping; condominiums; scuba diving; coin and stamp collecting; sky diving; vintage and classic automobile status symbols; gold credit cards; and on and on. Everybody wants to be in the swing—to outdo and outfashion other people. Jaguars outdo Cadillacs and Cadillacs top Chevys, chinchilla beats mink, a fashionable East Side brownstone tops a penthouse, and emeralds outshine rubies, which top diamonds.

Women's fashions, especially, are a continuing and influential phenomenon. It is said that they both reflect stock prices and influence market decisions. And why not? Doesn't the sex drive have an impact on just about everything?

Whose Idea Was This Anyway?

Mentioned in this context, fashion (the change in mode or style) refers to the prevailing style in women's dresses—specifically hemlines. The hemline theory, which undoubtedly will be assailed as a male chauvinist concept, contends there is a relationship between women's fashion and stock prices. Fashion changes are of course slower and less volatile than stock prices. Historically skirts have been the "lead" index; that is, changes in their direction, up or down, have occurred anywhere from three to eighteen months in advance of corresponding changes in stock prices.

Many people claim to have originated the hemline theory, but we believe the person responsible for the concept, or at least its fine-tuning, is Ira U. Cobleigh. An economist, he is an accomplished and prolific best-selling author and our coauthor on three past books. Having sold in excess of a million copies of over twenty books, Ira is clearly among "the fastest pens in the financial community!"

But back to business. Fashion was not really significant until after World War I. Before 1914, fashion clothes were custom-made, and dresses were not copied

widely or converted into mass production. Almost all
skirts were ankle length, while stock prices were of
concern to only a relatively small number of people.
Further, radical changes in style were not widely observed until the twentieth century. In the 1920s a revolution in both stocks and women's fashions developed,
as additional hundreds of thousands of people in the
United States discovered that they could afford both.
Volume production of common stocks and dresses
emerged.

New York City serves as the center of both popular
fashion (Paris aside) and finance. The rationale is that
higher incomes placed many New York women in a
position to dress more modishly. If women's fashions do
reflect the financial mood, it follows that the financial
markets will display strengths or weaknesses accordingly.

Testing the Theory

To put the hemline theory to the test we focused on the
most popular financial instrument (putting aside bonds,
government securities, bank deposits and loans, mortgages, leaseholds, mutual funds, etc.): common stock.
Stock prices are more publicized, readily measurable,
and more responsive to the mood and motion of the
economy than any other sector of the financial world.
So we decided to develop data and put them together
visually. We charted stocks, as measured by the Dow
Jones Industrial Average (DJIA), compared to dress
hemlines as the most visible and actively followed fashion phenomenon. As a result we have established a
continuing relationship between the two. (We are sorry
that we couldn't work waistlines or necklines into our
graph, but there is no evidence that plunging necklines
and plunging stock markets occur together.)

It is easy to get the statistics for stock prices. Hemline data is more difficult, since descriptions of the styles of many periods refer only to inches above or below the knee. Whose knee? A six-foot-tall woman would display, at knee length, an entirely different hemline level than a woman five feet, two inches. To make matters more complicated, hemlines are now measured by inches from the waist to the knee. To come to a common denominator, we selected a standard of a female five feet, seven inches tall and extrapolated, as best we could, the hemline as so many inches above the floor, so that varying lengths are directly comparable.

Do skirt lengths telegraph stock market direction? If you look at our pictorial graph for the sixty-nine-year period that is shown here, you'll see that skirts, for the most part, do just that. Hemlines rise before stocks do; ditto on the downside.

DON'T SELL TILL YOU SEE THE HEIGHTS OF THEIR THIGHS!

The data for the table we have prepared and the correlation between stock prices and hemlines originates around 1917. As we stated, it was about then that the public began to enter the stock market and become fashion conscious.

Early Movement

By looking at our graph and table, both titled "The Hemline Index of Stock Prices," you'll be able to see the relationship between skirt length and stock market action. Hemlines started down ahead of stocks in the 1920–21 depression. However, between 1925 and 1926, skirts rose to knee-high, a daring level by historic standards. As women's fashions showed more leg the stock

BULL MARKETS an
THE HEMLINE INDEX C

69 YEARS OF THE DOW-JONES
INDUSTRIAL AVERAGES

1922   1927   1932   1937   1942   1947   1952   1957

BARE KNEES!
STOCK PRICES

3,000

2,000

1,000

1962   1967   1972   1977   1982   1987   1991

Kieran Vogel

61

market too was being propelled to heights previously unheard of! There was significant directional indication of later stock market action in 1927, when skirts (of the flapper era) reached new highs (or new thighs). The year 1927 was a happy one: wide prosperity, animated speakeasies, the Charleston, introduction of the Chrysler auto, and stocks in a powerful upthrust. But late in 1927 the hemline peaked, and skirt lengths started a decline.

That downtrend in hemlines foreshadowed the market debacle of 1929 by almost two years. By the time the great crash arrived, skirts were, comparatively speaking, dragging along the floor. If only the hemline chart had been understood and its message read at that time. Investors would have known that dreary days for stocks were ahead and could have saved billions!

Beginning in late 1932 and pausing to correspond with the market slowdown in 1936–37, hemlines began to rise. They reached eight inches above the ground in 1939 and fifteen inches in 1940, indicating a market top. World War II followed next. Women's fashions and the stock market both went on hold for the duration. However, if you are old enough you will remember that wartime skirts were fairly short. They were styled for safety and utility for the wartime female work force in the defense plants. Also government restrictions on the production of cloth for civilians dictated skirt lengths.

After the War: Reestablishing the Pattern

Fashion reemerged after World War II, and hemlines were lower in 1947 than on VJ Day. Everyone expected a depression after World War II, and the lower skirt lengths foretold the descending stock market of 1949. The 1950s witnessed a general rise in the DJIA (checked in 1953 and again in 1956). The long dress of

THE HEMLINE INDEX OF STOCK PRICES

Year	Economy/ Hemline Description	Inches Hem to Floor	DJIA Median
1922		6.4	91
1927	Hemline peak	18.6	178
1932	Depression	9.8	65
1940–45	War years	14.5[1]	140[1]
1947	Postwar	8.1	175
1955	Rising trend	11.6	438
1967	Miniskirt	25.0	857
1978	Maxiskirt	15.0	825
1982	Miniskirt	24.3	924
1983	Consolidation	21.0	1157
1984	Miniskirt	24.0	1187
1987	Miniskirt	24.0	2361
1988	Consolidation	14.0	2031
1989	Consolidation	14.0	2468
1990	Miniskirt	25.0	2682
1991	Miniskirt	25.0	3168[2]

1. Average
2. Through December 31, 1991

Source: Fashion Institute of Technology

1950–51 gave way to rising hemlines, especially nota-
ble in 1954. By October 1961, skirts were close to
knee-high again, which gave warning that a dip was in
the cards. Ten months later a lull in the market developed. After a pause, skirts continued to rise once more
and topped off with the miniskirt. For a very brief
period the microskirt appeared; there literally was nowhere else to go! Shortly after, the DJIA peaked at a

closing high of 1001 on February 9, 1966. From there the market suffered a major correction.

All Dressed "Up" and Nowhere to Go: 1987's Black Monday

Lowered skirt lengths in 1970–71 predicted the market sell-off in 1974. Then, in 1975, the hemline started a slow rise, foretelling a rising market. Some consolidation in 1983 aside, hemlines continued to rise through the mid-1980s. In fall 1987, skirts and stocks were near record highs of twenty-four inches hem to floor. We were at the max. But whereas short skirts are definitely limited by modesty, stocks have no theoretical limit so they continued to soar off the chart to a DJIA in excess of 2700. The hemline theory warning was at full red alert.

On October 19, 1987, the market paid the price of a nonstop binge and crashed! The extent of the crash was beyond all the experiences of past market declines and collapses. Past market crashes were pillow fights compared to this baby! It was the first truly global crash. It raced through the world's financial markets. Over $600 million was wiped out from NYSE market values and from investors' portfolios on that Monday alone as the DJIA plunged 508 points on heavy volume.

It took a full year for the stock market to recover and only after severe damage was inflicted. In the two years following 1987's Black Monday, skirt lengths consolidated to an average fourteen inches from the floor—not quite maxiskirts but definitely conservative. The market action of 1988–89 was one of consolidation and regaining lost ground, with a near-miss "crashette" on Friday, October 13, 1989. So the signals were mixed, with a cautious bias.

All this changed again in 1990 and into fall 1991, when skirts again rose dynamically to an ogling level of twenty-five inches hem to floor, foretelling the new high ground of over 3000 on the DJIA in late 1991. By year-end 1991, the hemline again ascended to the mini level. At year-end December 31, 1991, the DJIA closed at 3168.

WHY DOES IT WORK? ANALYZING THE RELATIONSHIP

Thus the chronology of events documents a significant relationship between hemlines and stocks. But what's the motivation?

Both market swings and fashion changes are fueled as much by emotion as by money logic. High stocks and high skirts seem to reflect confidence, exuberance, hope, and happiness. Good times tend to spark amorous zeal, more animated girl-watching. And girl-watching seems more pleasurable when there is "more girl" to look at.

The sex drive and the money drive may originate from the same emotional sources. Stock dividends are more animated than margin calls. In developed nations, birth rates rise during prosperity and fall during depressions. Perhaps, too, a fashion trend toward lower skirts is a form of economic discipline, tending to make investors pay more attention to the business at hand when times are less prosperous!

Another observable phenomenon: higher skirts, symbolizing hope, confidence, and zest, are linked emotionally to livelier colors. Miniskirts feature a dazzling array of sporty colors—pastels, pinks, reds, yellows, and so on. Conversely, longer skirts are usually heavier and in darker colors: browns, dark grays, and blacks. In 1932, skirts were not only long but somber and funereal in color. If psychological spurs can be found in rising skirt levels, perhaps these attitudes can be reversed by longer skirts, cooling down romantic enthusiasm and ardor.

The constant emotional urge for a change in both financial and apparel fashion may rationalize the relationship we have tried to establish between hemlines and market heights—between sex and stocks. Our table may be of value as a barometer or cross-check on the market motions, and we are particularly impressed that the height of hemlines so clearly suggests a coming peak in stock prices.

PEEK AND VALLEY FORMULA!

The fashion watchers, therefore, rest their case on the general theory that hemlines precede, in motion and direction, the rise or fall of common stocks . . . a peek and valley formula. Hence the slogans "Bull Markets and Bare Knees!" and "Don't Sell till You See the Heights of Their Thighs!" Who knows where stocks will go if skirts get shorter? And how shall we chart a DJIA of 4000? By a navel engagement?

At any given time a variety of styles and fashions will be in evidence. Ladies fashions are a mixed bag today. Thus the hemline theory and the relationship between fashion and stocks may have to be modified to a measurement of how much girl there is to look at. We may see the birth of a new Wall Street folklore indicator: the ogling level predictor!

Members of the opposite sex will always watch each other. After all, it's just market research.

WALL STREET BELIEFS AND OTHER IRREVERENT INDICATORS

Be warned lest you think the hemline index of stock prices silly—an aberration visited upon the investment scene by a demented segment of the financial community. Before you ascribe the success of this phenomenon to chance and relegate it to the twilight zone, be advised that the hemline theory is but one of many Wall Street indicators . . . barometers of change that seem to work—in mysterious ways—a majority of the time. They are widely observed and can, over the short term, be significant.

These peculiarities of the market—particularly those dealing with the relationship between the sexes!—can be reliable predictors at times. For example, while the authors know of no formal statistical computation, there are those who believe that marital discord, as measured by the volume of divorce filings, is a clear indicator of tough economic times and foretells future stock market woes. When you consider that financial pressure is typically one of the prime catalysts bringing couples to the divorce courts, it makes a certain amount of sense to tie the decline of marital bliss to market discord.

Other observations and studies have focused on less likely indicators with a disturbing degree of success and compelling logic. The financial community is literally brimming with them. The more popular of these predictors range from calendar events tied to seasonal barometers, IRS taxes, holidays, January "dead-cat bounces," presidential elections, Super Bowl outcomes, animal population cycles, shopping cart inventories, used car sales, and musical lyrics—to name several. All have been documented to a minor or major degree by Wall Street's historians.

For us, however, the most dramatic of such indicators are those that measure the interest level and relationship between men and women. As ardor flourishes or wanes so will the stock market; so tune in and out of the stock market accordingly.

7
No One Line Works All the Time
(A Humble Suggestion for a Consistently Winning Strategy)

Back in the seventeenth century, Don Juan (a legendary nobleman from Seville, known thereabouts for his ceaseless and notably successful pursuit of fleshly delights) was attributed with the learned observation that

> "When close to honour's meek submission,
> 'Tis best to give, and thus at last to take."

As any investment professional (in New York that's anybody who takes his libations at Harry's more than twice a week) will tell you, that translates into twentieth-century English as "you gotta tell 'em what they want to hear." The trick, of course, is knowing what they want to hear at any given time . . . what sort of approach is *in* at the moment.

FADDISHNESS ON WALL STREET

Investment success regrettably seems to be prone to the same sort of faddishness. While there is no end to the number of plausible reasons why a stock or group of stocks should go up (e.g., low price/earnings ratio, high growth potential, small cap stock, low price/book ratio, high leverage, low leverage), the fact is that the stocks in vogue at any particular time generally share the same characteristic or group of characteristics.

There does not appear to be any logic to why that particular characteristic seems to drive the market at that particular time while stocks with equally plausible (but different) stories may languish. In the late sixties, for example, low-capitalization stocks were all the rage; they then stagnated for several years before bursting forth again in the middle to late seventies. The "nifty fifty" growth stocks of the early seventies managed to give the appearance of solid success to the popular market averages until they all began to unravel in 1973–74. Each particular formula for success will have its hour in the sun, but no single approach will work all the time. Worse, when an investment fad goes out of favor, it generally does so without much warning—and to the considerable anguish of its practitioners.

If you cannot know ahead of time which formula will work for the coming, say, year in helping you to score big on every investment outing, then what's a poor investor to do? Maybe the answer is to stop trying to score big and instead focus on scoring consistently.

Before offering up our candidate for the investment formula of the century, we need to put it into the proper context. Among the commodity traders who frequent Chicago's equivalent of Harry's, there is an old saying that only two rules apply in making money: Rule 1 is not to *lose* money, and Rule 2 is never to forget Rule 1. The point is, you don't need to score big—you just need to score repeatedly.

When you think about that, it sounds pretty good, doesn't it? The problem with scoring *big* is that it invariably entails a high level of risk, and the kind of investor reading this book—*our* kind of investor—is trying to have all the fun *without* all the risk. Which brings to mind the story of the young bull who, turning to the old bull, suggests running down the hill and grabbing one of the lovely young cows in the meadow. The old bull smiles, shakes his head, and counters with the suggestion to *walk* down the hill and take care of *all* the cows! So, for the old bulls among us, here is our suggestion for stock market success without ulcers.

FINDING THE LINE THAT WORKS: A STRATEGY FOR CONTINUED SUCCESS

Simple logic suggests that if you want to own stocks that will be in favor at any given point in time, they must share at least to a reasonable degree the characteristics that constitute the current fad. In other words, if low P/E is driving Wall Street wild with desire this year, then you want all your stocks to have low P/E—obviously. But if the turn-on is low debt levels, then you clearly want your holdings to show the strongest possible balance sheet. The same holds for price/book ratios, industry groupings, price/sales ratios, and so on.

The problem, of course, is that you don't know ahead of time which parameter to screen against. The really outstanding examples on any one parameter are not likely to be among the top candidates on many of the *other* parameters.

The answer: screen for *moderate* compliance with several key parameters rather than for outstanding examples along any single parameter. This will mean lots of singles and doubles and only the occasional home run, but the point is that you should always be in the game!

Sound too simple? Well, it isn't all that simple!

First, you do need a personal computer and access to a database that will allow you to screen for companies that meet your threshold on the several criteria you choose. Probably the least expensive database is Value Line. The basic service is available free at almost any public library. Assuming your public library is equipped with a computer, Value Line's proprietary screening software (Value Screen II) may be available as well. This software allows you to apply multiple screening criteria against Value Line's database of approximately 1,600 of the most widely traded stocks. It then lists the individual stocks that, at any level of screening, meet *all* of the designated criteria.

Obviously the greater number of criteria you impose, the smaller the number of companies that will meet all of those criteria. By the same token, the number of successful candidates will also be affected by the *severity* of the criteria measurement. More companies will pass your threshold for price/earnings ratio if that ratio is set at, say, 10 times trailing twelve-month earnings than if you insist on a tougher threshold of a price only 8 times earnings. Thus you can build a considerable amount of flexibility into this investment approach. The true art becomes finding the perfect balance between how many criteria you impose, how strict the measurement is on each one, and how many candidate stocks manage to run this gauntlet successfully. While there are many possible combinations the investor might use, here is one model that works! We decided to look for those companies that currently have:

- Low price/earnings (less than 11)
- Low price/book (less than 1.25)
- Low debt (less than 35 percent of total capitalization)

- Good earnings momentum (five-year earnings growth equal to or greater than 20 percent)
- Low price/sales (less than 75 percent)
- Moderate size (less than $500 million total capitalization)
- Dividend payments

Corporations that qualify will not be the ones making investment headlines today, nor will they be the institutional darlings being bid up ever higher. Rather than glamorous "Miss Universe" companies, these are the "Safe $ex" candidates. Appearing to be reasonably priced on *all* of a number of important criteria, they thus provide considerable downside protection as well as the potential for future capital appreciation in line with the success of the underlying companies themselves. Whichever investment approach happens to be in vogue over the coming months, these companies are likely to qualify as players. They may not be the absolute leaders, but they should certainly be around for the finals.

While you may fiddle with the individual components of the screening model, this basic approach affords a rational, consistent "line" to use in *any* investment environment. It should serve you well in the ongoing struggle to find worthwhile companions for your portfolio.

8
The Rhythm Method
(Infallible Stock Charting . . . Almost!)

We find no greater evidence of the emotional empathy driving both stock prices and sex than stock price charting. Both are driven by the passion and momentum of the moment and predict future events accordingly. The behavior of a suitor in the heat of pursuit is predictable (or so it is thought); the same for the flip side—rejection or the cooling of ardor. Well, sometimes yes, sometimes no. Usually the outcome is not quite that which was predicted.

Stock charting, referred to as technical analysis, attempts to predict stock market and stock price behavior based on the way two lovers or past lovers might behave. Just as the lovers' current attitude toward one another affects their relationship and actions, so it is believed that investors' love (or hate) affair with a stock will affect its price movement. So far so good. However, many models assume that price trends will continue for periods beyond the short-term perspective of most investors. When emotional empathy theories are extended to predict future performance, they become dangerous. This is particularly true when charts are extrapolated over longer and longer periods.

As you can tell, we are not totally enamored with stock charting as a reliable method for stock selection; we liken its reliability to that of the rhythm method (for more amorous pursuits). Neither is foolproof, but one must work with the tools at hand. As a sizable population of stock pickers live by the charts, you need to be able to interpret chart patterns as their followers would. After all, we are all in favor of the search for stocks that outperform the market, and stock price cycles can be important to the price of many individual stocks.

Stock price trends are usually explained as reactions to the staggered spread of new information entering the market, such as an earnings report, a plant closing, or a product introduction. Superior investment performances can be achieved by early recognition of a trend change in the price of a stock. Both the stock market and individual stocks exhibit chart formations that are common signals. But the signals can be inconsistent, misleading, and subject to interpretation. Furthermore, many charting methods are lagging or coincidental indicators, confirming what has already happened. Thus peaks and troughs are so difficult to determine that the best to be expected is to profit by capturing the middle part of a bullish or bearish trend.

One nice thing about stock charting is that it is popular. As such there is a current chart (and technical opinion) available on just about any worthwhile stock in existence. Most brokerage firms have technical skills and will, on demand, supply reams of research on the market and on stocks. And on charts, just like sex, everybody thinks he or she is an expert. Scary stuff!

TIME TO MAKE A MOVE? TECHNICAL SIGNALS FOR BUYING AND SELLING

Just as you cannot fathom the chemistry of your attraction to a member of the opposite sex, charts cannot fundamentally explain the reasons a stock will change. However, if enough practitioners utilize chart formations, they become self-fulfilling prophecies and cause price changes when investors react to changes in opinion. The trick is to know when to make your move. Self-validating, like a honeymoon, lasts only too briefly. Then reality sets in, and the emotional excess of the moment is reckoned with.

What follows are the basic chart formations that make up the bulk of the technician (chartist) craft. While literally tons of texts have been written on technical analysis, there are but a few vital stock and market indicators. You may find some of the chart patterns characterized by sensuous nomenclature—further evidence of the connection between sex and money! Here most of all, you should practice Safe $ex. No matter how good that chart (or body) looks to you, exercise care and reason and, above all, protect yourself!

Cumulative Advance-Decline Line

A major tool used to forecast breadth of the overall stock market is the cumulative advance-decline line. Daily and weekly it measures the number of stocks that have advanced in price, subtracted from the number of stocks that declined in price. This is expressed on a chart by an advance-decline line (A/D line). The A/D line is a cumulative total of the net number of advancing stocks versus declining stocks (normally for the New York Stock Exchange). For example, if on any given day the number of advancing stocks were 1000 and the number of declining stocks were 300, the A/D line would be increased by 700. Conversely, if 300 stocks advanced and 1000 declined the A/D line would be decreased by 700. The direction of change is more meaningful than the magnitude of change. A bearish signal is given when the advance-decline is headed downward even though the market as measured by the popular indexes continues higher.

New Highs–New Lows Technique

Another tool used to recognize a change in the market trend is the new highs–new lows technique. To formulate it, subtract the number of stocks reaching new lows from those reaching new highs and divide the remainder by the total number of issues traded. A sustained decline in the new highs–new lows while the market indexes continue to rise is a bearish indicator. Information and graphs on new high–new low indicators are provided in the *Wall Street Journal* and *Barron's* as well as in the financial sections of many newspapers.

Support Level

The clearest sell signal for both market and individual stocks is a drop below a market level or stock price that is considered a major "support" level—a level at which past declines have repeatedly ended and at which strong buying has caused the stock market or stock price to recover. Penetration of a support level is evidence that a stock that previously attracted buyers no longer does so. Another rather obvious strong indication that a stock is headed down occurs when the overall market is rising and trading volume in a stock is heavy but its price fails to advance, or when a stock is not making gains similar to others in its industry group.

Resistance Level

A strong buy signal for the market and individual stocks is a breakout above a market resistance level or stock price plateau that is considered a major resistance area—a level at which past rises have repeatedly ended and at which strong selling caused the market or stock price to decline. Penetration of a resistance level is evidence that buyers are being attracted.

Head and Shoulders

Another popular technical signal is a classic sell signal—the head and shoulders—a stock price formation where the chart rises, then declines and again rises higher than before, followed by another decline, then a smaller rise. From the third rise, the price trend is expected to go downward. The converse, a reverse head and shoulders, is deemed to be a buy signal.

Spike

The spike occurs when, in the briefest of trading sessions, a stock soars to a peak and immediately begins an even sharper retreat. Very bearish indicator.

Broken Long-Term Trendline

The broken long-term trendline occurs when an established trendline of price behavior flattens and either declines or rises. It is a strong sell or buy signal, respectively.

Chart A, on AW Computer Systems, Inc., illustrates the above three chart patterns—the head and shoulders, the spike, and the broken long-term trendline—in this stock's trading from the end of 1986 through 1991. See the following page.

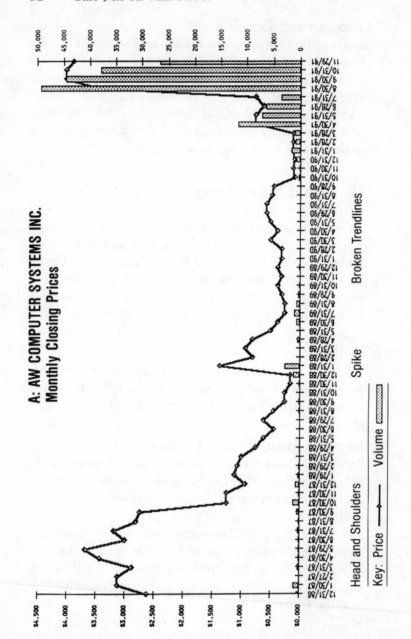

A: AW COMPUTER SYSTEMS INC.
Monthly Closing Prices

Head and Shoulders   Spike   Broken Trendlines

Key: Price ——— Volume ▨▨▨

B: APPLE COMPUTER INC.

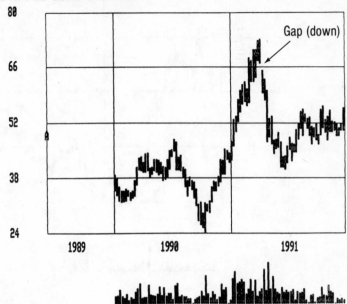

DECEMBER 1991

Gap

The gap (see chart B) occurs when a stock trades measurably away from its last trade. This infrequent occurrence is significant. Price gaps, the technicians preach, are a symptom of excess. Gaps are almost always closed in subsequent trading. A gap down is bearish. A gap up is bullish. Both are treacherous.

Wedge Pattern

Stock prices form a pattern with declining tops and rising bottoms until a wedge is formed (see chart C). A buy signal.

C: CARRINGTON LABORATORIES INC.

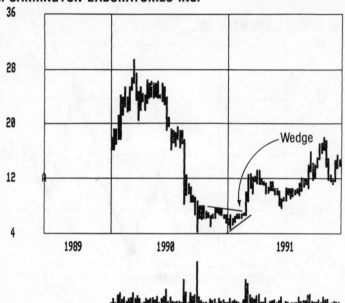

D: PETRIE STORES CORPORATION

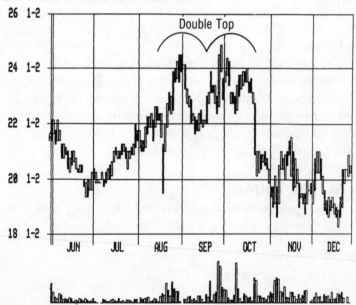

Double Tops

Double tops on a chart, such as in chart D, indicate that a stock price has trouble advancing. It is a bearish signal. The pattern develops due to an approximate equal distribution of demand and supply. (Note: If you think we've forgotten our promise of "sensuous nomenclature" try the traditional definition of this picture!) The chart resembles a double mound with a valley in the middle. The second mound is the significant one since it reveals that the stock price action was insufficient to surmount previous peaks. The volume of shares traded is usually lower during the formation of the second top. Also a double top can coincide with a break in the uptrend line.

Triple Tops

A pattern of three failed attempts to break out of a specific price level is called a triple top (see chart E).

E: AMOCO CORPORATION

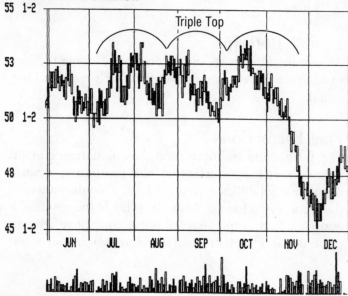

DECEMBER 1991

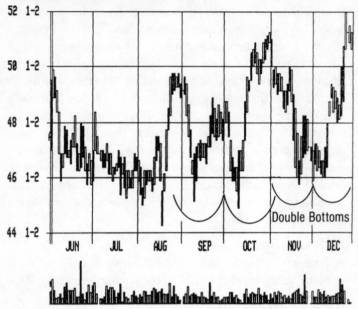

F: EMERSON ELECTRIC COMPANY

DECEMBER 1991

Double Bottoms
As you might expect, the reverse of a double top can exist. A double bottom (see chart F) is a technical buy signal.

Flag Formations
Flag formations are interesting. Just as someone might flag you to get your attention, this formation, a pause during an established trend, "flags" a continuation of the trend or a change. Actually a flag is the result of a consolidation, typically following an above-average price move. Flag patterns (see chart G) appear when

G: ALLIED RESEARCH CORPORATION

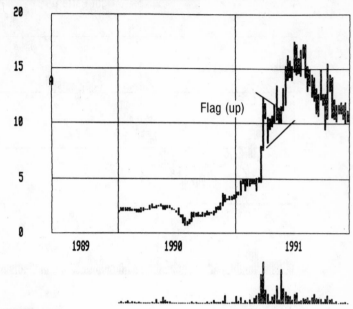

Flag (up)

1989   1990   1991

DECEMBER 1991

the trend is up and in the opposite direction when the trend is down. A flag for a downtrending stock will have the consolidation pointing upward, in a direction counter to the forecast downtrend of the stock.

Special Chart Patterns

Tight Versus Loose

Generally, tighter price patterns exhibiting small variations in price from week to week, as shown in chart H, are preferred. Stocks with price patterns that are extremely wide and loose (see chart I) are not attractive.

H: PHILADELPHIA ELECTRIC COMPANY

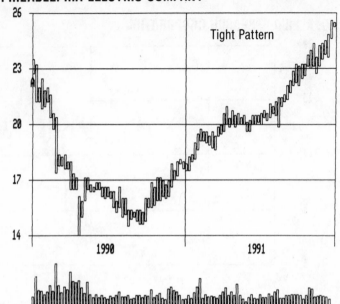

Tight Pattern

30-DEC-91

I: PET INC.

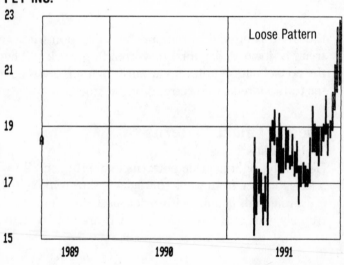

Loose Pattern

J: PREMARK INTERNATIONAL INC.

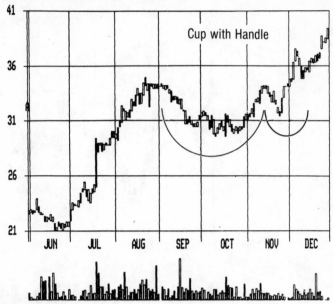

Cup with Handle

DECEMBER 1991

Cup with Handle

A familiar buy signal, the cup-with-handle formation builds over time (up to a year) and lasts three to five months. Basically, a downward stock price drift forms a rounded bottom giving the appearance of a cup, as in chart J. This is followed by a short period of a few weeks that duplicates the pattern at the rim of a cup with a shallow replay of the cup formation. Hence the handle is formed. The technician's theory is that a sound formation has been created for the next advance. Cups without handles have a higher failure.

K: GTE CORPORATION

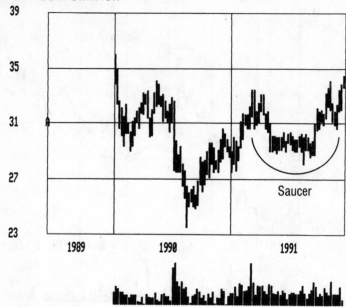

DECEMBER 1991

Saucer

What would a cup be without a saucer? So we have a stock formation similar to the cup but somewhat longer and more shallow (see chart K). Where's the handle? Well, don't worry. The handle is there; it's just invisible. It exists, you see, in terms of how long the saucer pattern took to form. Don't you just love it?

WATCHING THE MOVES

So there you have it—all you ever wanted to know about technical analysis but were afraid to ask. When you come down to it, reading charts is like ogling the opposite sex. Watch the moves and you'll see the signals clearly. You don't have to be a rocket scientist to understand the obvious. The object of your observation will signal intent and direction as clearly as will the pattern of stock price movement. Just remember, be guided by the moment and don't get locked into long-term prognostication.

9
Do You *Really* Want a Virgin?
(*A Bottom-Line Approach to Initial Public Offerings*)

Webster's Ninth New Collegiate Dictionary defines *virgin* as free of impurity or stain; being used or worked for the first time; initial, first, fresh, unspoiled. As it refers to humans, it is defined as a person who is absolutely chaste.

Do you really want a virgin, be it a companion or an investment? Well, why not? Doesn't everyone want the newest, to be among the relatively first few to have one (or in the case of a man or woman—the very only one to be first), to be at the head of the line, to be enraptured with the rush of possessing the unsullied—that which has not been altered by activity and use by others? Conventional wisdom holds that new is the way to go. New is unused and therefore lasts longer. It is the top of the line, a better performer, dependable, and so on. In all things, the line of reasoning continues, new is best. Not to be new is to be second-hand and second-rate.

Well, what you want and what's good for you are

often two different things, usually extreme opposites. Our advice is to forget conventional wisdom. If it was any good, the world would be chock-full of happiness and wealth. Instead ask those who have been there. If honest, they'll admit that new, or first, is not what it is cracked up to be. Further they'll tell you that in virgin territory all the problems are up-front, with little reward. In truth, new (virgin) is untested, unpracticed, unpredictable, not reliable, not broken in. In the investment world, it is typically the most expensive emotionally and financially. Finally, as often as not, what is represented as new is in fact "old hat" merely dressed up to appear otherwise.

THE BRIDE WORE WHITE

The bride—or, if you will, virgin—in the stock market is the privately owned company making it to the public stock market. This is accomplished by selling ownership in the company to the public and having the shares trade afterward, either over the counter or on an exchange such as the New York Stock Exchange or the American Stock Exchange. This is commonly referred to as "going public." We don't know about you, but the phrase "going public" has always had a negative connotation for us. It implies that some element, concealed until recently, is now out in the open to the chagrin and general distress of those involved. In this case the negative implication may well be deserved.

The procedure by which a firm enters the public market is the "initial public offering," better known as the IPO. The ceremony at which the IPO takes place is known as the underwriting. This is when the investment banker gives the "bride" away to the public, for an outrageous fee. On one side of the aisle is the bride's family, represented by the underwriting syndicate, selling group, brokers, and selling shareholders such as officers, employees of the firm, entrepreneurs, venture capital investors, and hedge funds (short sellers)—in other words all those who would take your money in exchange for shares they hold in the company or for commissions and fees paid to them for selling those shares to you. On the other side of the aisle is the sheep pen . . . that is, those members of the public who are buying all these shares and the hype that goes along with it.

The reception is the celebration that lasts for the briefest of times until the underwriting syndicate is dissolved. During that very brief period (as long as a day or two or as short as a few minutes) the underwriters will hold a syndicate bid out for limited quantities of stock. When that bid is gone, the party is truly over. The stock, just like the newlyweds, must find its own way in the real world after that. Often the stock will trade at a discount to the price at which the public just bought it.

Axiom: There is rarely a honeymoon period for the IPO stock.

A STACKED DECK

By now it should be abundantly clear that we don't like or trust IPOs. We'll spell out the good reasons in a moment. For starters, though, when pitched to buy in on the ground floor with an IPO, remember two things: (1) If this is a hot deal, why isn't it already sold out, and why are you being offered an opportunity to buy in? The risk is in direct relation to the quantity of an IPO stock available to you for purchase. The more stock available, the greater the chance for loss. (2) Put aside the more well-publicized success stories of earlier IPOs. They are so few as to be virtually meaningless. They are the exceptions that prove the rule. And if your broker tells a recent IPO success story, ask why you weren't offered any. That'll be an interesting answer!

But enough of this cynicism. Let's get down to hard facts. There are seven very basic reasons why the IPO as a rule doesn't make it for the investor.

1. Everybody Has a Finger in the Pie but You

Remember what side of the aisle you are on. You are disadvantaged. You're shelling out the money, and the other guy is raking it in. The investment banker is selling stock to you that moments before cost him up to 10 percent less than he is selling it for. Also, depending upon the structure of the transaction, he has also been paid an unaccountable expense allowance (a thinly disguised method of raising his compensation package), five-year warrants, probably a long-term cash retainer, and a paying seat on the board of directors.

Also remember the lawyers, accountants, consultants, and last but not least the financial printer, with whose product, the prospectus, you are solicited. Finally, there is the broker, anxious for the generous commissions that new issues generate, who will pitch the offerings with special zeal. All this adds up to a tidy sum.

Somebody has to pay for all this. So it is priced into the stock you are buying. You are paying all these people's fees! And they are paid up front, whereas you have to make it in the stock market over time. You are coming up from behind, and the odds are the catch-up will be some time in coming.

2. All Brides Are Beautiful. Yeah, Sure!

The preparation and hype that go into a wedding pale in comparison to the promotion of an IPO. The market for an IPO is controlled, and the price is contrived and wholly arbitrary. Aside from the aforementioned costs built into the pricing of the IPO, the base price is determined by the seller (better known as the issuer, or company) and the lead underwriter. Pricing, like beauty, is in the eyes of the beholder. The price is set at whatever the market (you, the investor) will bear.

If the issuer is an operating company, the price may exhibit some passing relationship to assets and earnings. Not much, but some. If the IPO is a start-up or emerging company, the price is pure fiction.

The sellers (company owners) are understandably eager to get top dollar for their holdings. Consequently they are generally smart enough to sell out at a time when business is about as good as it is going to get. A recent study on the subject shows that of companies making IPOs in the past four or five years, more than half have since posted earnings declines; one in seven had a loss within a year; and about 70 percent exhibited a marked deceleration of earnings growth. In other words, buyers of IPOs usually are buying in at the top.

In any case the IPO will be priced as high as possible. Under these circumstances the buyer can hardly hope to do more than come out even.

3. You'll Be the Last One to Know

The textbook purpose of an IPO is to bring credibility and public exposure to the issuer (the company) and to raise the capital needed to grow the business. If you believe that, you probably still believe in the tooth fairy!

While the IPO does bring needed cash to the company, it also establishes a public market for the stock—thus providing the founders, entrepreneurs, management, seed money investors, and so on, a means by which they can cash out. Some will sell portions immediately by piggybacking their shares on the IPO. Others will wait in the wings, looking for an opportunity to sell in the future.

Suspect the worst when entrepreneurs, founders, and other insiders sell their own stock in a company's initial public offering. This is particularly true if a substantial amount of the shares in the offering are being sold by management and insiders rather than by the company itself. Take a jaundiced view. The insiders have had their fun and are checking out, while you're just coming to the party. Talk about being secondhand!

4. Seeds of Destruction

All IPOs have within them the seeds of their own destruction. The very mechanics of the underwriting procedure are such that the odds of a price decline are overwhelming.

Remember always the underwriting and selling group has only one purpose in mind . . . to sell the deal! That's what they do. That's how they make a living. The aftermarket price of the stock (the level at which the supply and demand in the marketplace fix the price following the underwriting) is of secondary, if any, real interest to them, lip service to the contrary notwithstanding.

Now, here comes the real killer! In order to make the deal happen, underwriters will include in their selling group brokerage firms that will short the stock to the syndicate bid. Remember, the selling group of brokers is buying the stock at a discount to the IPO selling price and therefore can cover with a built-in profit. Some weaker underwriters will sell to groups that short the stock on the offering. The latter are typically hedge funds, secure in the knowledge that IPOs usually decline in price, who will sell short on any strength in the IPO and cover with the IPO shares.

The seeds of destruction are sown. All the ingredients are in place for the IPO stock price to move down rather than up.

5. They Don't Know How to Behave in Public

Nothing is more parochial than a virgin. Private companies are no different. Preoccupied with their privacy for years, they have difficulty being in bed with a partner, namely you, the public shareholder. No more secrecy! The most intimate financial details about the company, its senior officers, its directors, and so forth, will be subject to disclosure and scrutiny. A good example is the entrepreneur (who shall remain nameless) who became an instant millionaire with his company's IPO and, in a subsequent press interview, complained that he had lost his privacy. Poor baby!

Furthermore the board of directors and management are now accountable to their partner. No more nights out with the boys or girls. No more private-company mentality with generous perks for the owners. Growth, earnings, and dividends are expected and demanded. Those promises (projections) that were so easy to make before the nuptials (the underwriting) must be delivered.

Adjustment is difficult. As often as not, the management doesn't make it. It is not uncommon for a new management team eventually to replace the first string. Even well-meaning founders who recognize the need for delegating and building a management team usually find themselves unable to pull it off. In any case, the IPO investor who experiences major management transition is likely to see the stock go lower before it settles in.

6. And They're So Young!

The bulk of the IPOs are underage. Put aside the unborn (start-ups, development-stage companies, and concept businesses) and you will still find that the bulk of the IPO companies are under ten years of age . . .

mere babies by most measures. Further they are still living at home with Mommy and Daddy. Most still have at least one founder at the helm. Some have entire families of founders employed throughout the company as well. These are commonly known as "privately owned public companies." Believe us, you don't want to be in on one of these. They are accidents waiting to happen.

7. Old Age and Skill Will Overcome Youth and Treachery Every Time

Nothing but nothing beats experience. We've witnessed far too many IPOs, flush with newfound wealth courtesy of the underwriting, burn their way right through the capital raised. Sometimes the IPO slips into oblivion. Sometimes it can't get off the ground. Sure, an occasional one will make it. But the stock rarely lives up to the expectations expressed at the time of the underwriting. Give us an experienced management team, with years in the saddle and a public track record, anytime.

REPAIRED VIRGINS

Although more than a few companies would masquerade as born-again virgins, there isn't any such animal. Public offerings of stock for the second, third, or fourth time, or even more, are known as secondary offerings, or secondaries. The sellers would have you believe that these are outstanding opportunities. Control your desire. They can be more hazardous than the IPOs.

Most of the preceding commentaries on IPOs apply to secondaries as well, with the possible exception of secondary offerings of very large firms, such as public utilities. However, there is another threat to your financial health brought about by secondary offerings. Wall Street is a slave to the forces of supply and demand in a free market system. You don't have to be a rocket scientist to recognize the oversupply condition that a secondary stock offering creates and the inevitable decline of the stock price that results.

When all is said and done, we were all virgins at one time in our personal and investment lives. Maybe as a personal experience it was fun. The authors don't remember—it's been too long ago, and we don't *want* to remember! But in investments, virginity is not something you want to make a career of. It is definitely a case of more trouble (risk) than it is worth (reward).

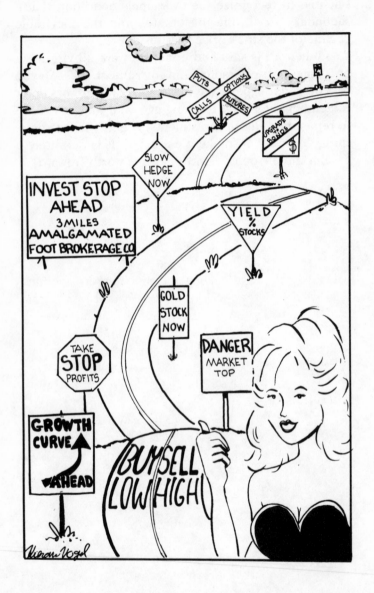

10
Going All the Way
(The Art of Taking Profits)

Investing one's hard-earned and much-harder-accumulated cash is a very serious business, and has a great deal in common with the equally sober business of relating to members of the opposite sex. Both are characterized as being tense, deadly in earnest, extremely emotional, intimate, complex, and fast-moving. Sex and the stock market share the same primeval drive: the gratification of needs and wants.

As much as these two pursuits have in common, there are two major differences. First, from the very beginning, unlike serious social relationships, commitments on Wall Street are made to be broken. Not even lip service should be given to lifelong investment affairs—love is for people, not for stocks! People who fall in love with a stock are almost always painfully scorned by the market.

Second, relationships between women and men have two viewpoints—those of each partner. No matter how much each may believe they share the same objective, the harsh reality is that neither fully understands the other's point of view and motivation. In fact they probably don't fully understand their *own* objectives, much less their partner's!

Nevertheless, lifelong contractual commitments are entered into. Long-term goals are set. Resources, both time and material, are committed. But there can be no misunderstanding of an investment objective. Making money is the one and only goal! This brings us to the need to go all the way on Wall Street—not just to get in but to get out and pin down profits.

THE PROFIT-TAKING DILEMMA

The three major areas of the investment process are (1) what to buy, (2) when to buy, and (3) when to sell. In today's fast-paced Wall Street the skill of making money in the stock market is surpassed only by the art of hanging on to profits once made. This chapter views a spectrum of guidelines to those conditions that make a stock a sale.

Generally the proper use of capital is to preserve it and to make it grow. Investments will ultimately flow to areas that grow fastest, provided the safety factors are about equal. Aside from the instances when liquidation of an investment is based upon personal need, taking profits should be the result of adjusting risk and opportunity.

When should the investor managing his own stock portfolio sell? As with the entire investment process, the correct answer is based on elementary logic. Briefly, price trends of individual stocks are usually explained as reactions to the staggered timing of the spread of new information entering the market; superior profits are achieved by early recognition of a trend change. Also, peaks and troughs are difficult to determine, and catching the absolute top or bottom is very hard to do. The best you can expect is to profit by capturing the middle part of a bullish or bearish trend.

All investors have heard the classic tale of the investors who bought and held what was to become IBM. These authors have never met such an individual (although we concede that there may have been a few— even fairy tales have some basis in fact). However, we do know of scores among acquaintances and professionals who have failed to bail out of situations despite the strongest sell signals. These are present-day, true-life horror stories! To prevent such disasters, you must be unceasingly aware of the need to sell, setting objectives going in and constantly reviewing them against the following criteria for selling.

CRITERIA FOR SELLING

It is assumed that a serious investor has undertaken due diligence in examining the worth of the investment as covered in Chapter 2. Therefore the what and when to buy have been established. Attention now moves to following the investment and timing a profitable exit.

Having reviewed the historic perspective and example of past market and stock price behavior, the benchmarks and signals for selling can be summarized in a relatively few rules and guidelines. Decisions for selling are based upon fundamental, technical (charting), and philosophical considerations.

Fundamental Considerations

Fundamental reasons for unloading a stock occur when the guidelines discussed in Chapter 2 are violated. Key indicators are:

1. *Excessive price/earnings ratios.* P/Es may be measured absolutely and relatively. In absolute terms

and by any standard, a P/E ratio above 20 could be a target for correction. This is particularly true if the P/E of a stock has risen 50 percent or more in a relatively short time. The P/E of market indices similarly measures the overall market's exposure. Historically the Dow Jones Industrial Average (DJIA) at 18 times earnings is blowing a whistle that the market is peaking. As the DJIA goes, eventually the majority of stocks will follow. Absurd heights of P/E have provided urgent sell signals in the past.

2. *Excessive ratios of price to book value.* The price/book value ratio can also reflect excesses, although it is a more meaningful indicator relative to the market than to individual equities. This is because high-growth stocks will legitimately outpace their book value quickly. Nevertheless glamour stocks are vulnerable to overall market correction, and it is wise to consider the DJIA book value a dependable benchmark of bullish and bearish sentiment. Generally when the DJIA climbs to a material premium to book value (80 percent or more) it is preparing to sell off.

3. *Extremes in growth rates.* Growth rates of sales, earnings, dividends, and financial strength all figure in programming the sale of stocks. There are two popular theories for evaluation of growth stocks. One says that a stock can sell at a 50 percent premium to the P/E of the DJIA if its earnings at least double within five years. Another, more aggressive approach postulates that a stock is entitled to trade at a P/E equivalent to its growth rate. Both approaches are more liberal than traditional standards but can be used except when taken to the extreme of a price over forty times earnings! No matter how exciting the prospects for the future may be, a stock driven to such excessive levels is a candidate for

liquidation. Other key signals for selling decisions are significant deterioration in a company's fundamentals—its sales growth, profitability, financial health, competitive position, and prospects for its industry. A company can lose its investment allure just as quickly, if not even *more* quickly, than it gained the allure.

4. *Unfulfilled Anticipations.* Sell if an anticipated favorable development—product unveiling, takeover bid, earnings pop, whatever—doesn't occur. If the blessed event doesn't come to pass, get out. Also, if the expected does happen and the stock doesn't react, either in anticipation or in reaction, unload immediately!

Technical Considerations

In Chapter 8 we discussed some of the stock behavior patterns technical analysts look for. By studying price data and trading volume, technical analysts can detect sell signals both for stocks and for the overall market.

The two major tools used to track market breadth and trend changes, respectively, are the cumulative advance-decline line and the new highs–new lows technique. For a full description of these indicators, you can review Chapter 8. Basically, a bearish signal is given when either of these measurements is headed downward although the usual market indicators continue to climb.

As we have already pointed out, technical signals (both buy and sell) are readily available and so widely heeded that they tend to be self-validating.

Philosophical Considerations

Philosophical and sentiment indicators that tell you when to sell, take a profit, or cut a loss are as valid a part of the philosophy of money management as are the fundamental and technical indicators. In today's fast-moving financial markets it is not prudent to ponder the sell decision for too long. That's why selling at the right time is such a difficult thing to do and why, in recent years, philosophical and sentiment indicators have come into vogue.

Market and stock barometers that measure what corporate insiders (company officers and directors) are doing, odd-lot activity, retail (individual) cash and margin account trading, short-selling patterns, institutional activity, and the bearishness or bullishness of market advisory letters are sentiment indicators. All are aimed at pinpointing broad market direction. Insider trading indicators signal investors to follow the leader, while the others (such as short selling by the public) are "contrary" indicators, which suggest the investor should go in the opposite direction.

The trading patterns and other such sell signals covered are not necessarily foolproof, nor are they reliable predictors in every situation. However, they are widely observed and at times can be significant. They should be used in conjunction with all the other investment tools when you contemplate an exit decision.

The stock market is a cruel place, with no sympathy for those who doggedly hold on to a loser, hoping it will climb back up. Once a stock or industry group falls from favor, the way down can be steep and long. When you buy a stock it's a sound practice to have some idea of the price at which you would sell if the stock is a winner—or bail out if it's a loser. By shirking sell decisions, not only is an investor *not* playing it safe, he's taking the biggest risk of all.

11
Pillow Talk
(The Language of Investing)

Communication is key in dealing effectively and productively in every relationship, whether it be a romantic liaison, infatuation between two people, a business negotiation, or a stock transaction. How often has a couple split up because of a carelessly uttered word or two or for something not said? A business deal can also collapse due to the improper expression of a party's true intent.

Nowhere is the need for precise communication greater than on Wall Street. When attempting to evaluate an investment opportunity or interpret a shareholder's communication, you must be able to separate the wheat from the chaff. You must pluck from the rhetoric the true meaning conveyed. But most of all, it is of paramount importance that your instructions be precise when you place a buy or sell order with your broker. Your order cannot be subject to misinterpretation. Putting your foot in your mouth on Wall Street is more than embarrassing, it's downright expensive!

To help you communicate effectively in the language of investing, we offer as a guide, rather than the typical glossary, a trilogy of Common Financial Terms, The Language of Order Placing, and Financial Buzzwords and Irreverent Wall Street Terminology.

COMMON FINANCIAL TERMS

Accumulation: The earliest phase in a bull market. A significant uptrend. (This is love at first sight—opening the mating season!)

American Stock Exchange: The second major securities exchange in New York; sometimes called "The Curb."

Analyst: An investment professional who evaluates securities and market trends. (The alleged expert and consummate professional—yeah, sure.)

Annual Report: The official statement and summary of assets, liabilities, earnings, and net worth and progress (if any) of a company, covering a fiscal or calendar year. (You can read all about this beauty in Chapter 2.)

Averages: The various barometers of stock price trends. Best known are the Dow Jones Industrial Average; Standard & Poor's 425 Industrial Average; New York Stock Exchange (NYSE) Common Stock Index; and the New York Times Average of 50 stocks. (Averages provide sort of a weather report—and are about as reliable.)

Balance Sheet: A financial statement defining the assets, liabilities, capital, and net worth of a corporation on a specified date. (Again, you can read all about this in Chapter 2.)

Bear: An investor or analyst who anticipates a stock market decline; a stock market pessimist.

Bid and Asked: A quotation of the best price at which to buy a stock, bond, or futures or options contract; conversely the lowest-priced offering of the same at a given moment. (Watch yourself on this one! Beware the broker who "cuffs a quote"—shoots from the hip and gives an inaccurate quote—on which you may base a decision.)

Blue Chip: Investor slang for the common stock of a major company that has a long record of earnings and dividends. In years past, blue chips were considered safe and conservative investments. Experience in the last two decades has proved otherwise. Quality stocks (blue chips), history teaches, can lose just as big and maybe bigger than a wallflower stock. For example, IBM, the bluest of the blue, traded at a 1991 February high of 139¾; as of February 14, 1992, it closed at 89¾! (Don't let a stock's pretty face or a deep blue hue lead you astray, into a false sense of security.)

Book Value: All the assets of a company less all liabilities and the par value of preferred stocks (if any), divided by the number of common shares outstanding.

Broker: A securities dealer associated with a member of a stock exchange or a broker/dealer firm, who executes buy and sell orders for a commission. Known by many other labels such as account executive, registered representative, and financial planner. (A broker by any other name is still a broker!)

Bull: An investor or analyst who anticipates the stock market will rise; a market optimist.

Capital Assets: Land, factories, equipment, transport equipment, and all the hard assets owned by a company. (The nitty gritty.)

Capital Gain or Loss: Profit or loss resulting from selling a security (or other asset). (Proof of the pudding.)

Capitalization: The total of all securities (debt and equity) issued by a company.

Cash Flow: The net income of a company (for a given period), to which are added noncash expense items such as depreciation, depletion, amortization charges, and nonrecurring charges to reserves; frequently stated "per share" by analysts. Cash flow is a measure of a company's financial health. For example, a company may have poor per share earnings but have a strong cash flow.

Charts: Graphic portrayals of statistical data about price, volume, and trends in different stocks in the hope of indicating the future direction of stock prices and/or the market in general. (About as reliable as the rhythm method!)

Chicago Board of Options Exchange: The exchange on which most options are traded. (Not for the faint of heart; ice water in your veins helps in playing this game.)

Commission: The fee charged by a broker for execution of an order. (No comment.)

Common Stock: The ownership or equity interest in a corporation, with a claim on assets or earnings after the deduction of debt and preferred stock (if any). This is a theoretical value; you don't get a chance to collect unless your company is going bankrupt—then stand at the end of the line!

Convertible: A debt instrument or preferred stock that may under certain conditions be exchanged for common stock, usually in the same company. (Sometimes playing it safe pays. A properly priced convertible with an acceptable yield can be a safer bet than a common stock. Alas, like a good date, they're few and far between.)

Current Assets: Assets in cash, receivables, short-term securities, and items collectible and convertible into cash within a year.

Current Liabilities: What a company owes that must be paid within a year.

Current Ratio: Ratio of current assets to current liabilities. (At the evening's end can your date pay the tab and still have cash for the cab ride home?)

Cyclical Stocks: The stocks of companies and businesses whose revenues and earnings tend to fluctuate with the business cycle or seasonal patterns.

Debenture: The long-term debt obligation of a corporation.

Delisting: Removal of a security from trading on a stock exchange. (Big trouble!)

Discount Rate: The percentage charged by the Federal Reserve Bank on loans to its member banks.

Distribution: Cresting phase of a bull market. (Time to sell!)

Dividend: A payment authorized by the board of directors of a corporation, either in cash or stock, pro rata among shareholders; usually a distribution made from current or past profits. (Payback time.)

Dow Jones Industrial Average (DJIA): The combined price index of stocks for thirty of the most important corporations in the United States. (The few lead the many.)

Dow Theory: An attempt to project stock market trends on the basis of the correlated past market action of thirty industrial and twenty transportation stocks. (About as meaningful as footprints in the sand. What's behind you don't count; it's what's up front that deserves your attention.)

Equity: The interest in a company represented by

shares of its common or preferred stocks.

Ex Dividend: When a stock is without the right to receive the latest declared dividend. An ex dividend stock is worth less, so its price declines.

Ex Dividend Date: The date on which investors who own stock will receive a dividend. Those who have sold the stock short must pay out the dividend to the owner of the stock.

Exercise: The process by which an options buyer notifies the seller of his or her intention to take delivery of the underlying instrument (in the case of a call option) or sell the instrument (in the case of a put option). (Put up or shut up.)

Exercise Price: The price at which an option entitles the holder to purchase the underlying stock; also known as the strike price.

Expiration: The date and time after which an option may no longer be exercised. (Too late!)

Extrinsic Value: The amount by which an option's premium (the fee paid to the seller of the option contract) exceeds its intrinsic value (the difference between the exercise price and the market price); also known as time value.

Federal Reserve Board: The quasi-government agency controlling the supply and price of money and regulating installment credit and margin loans.

Float: The amount of stock in public hands, excluding insider holdings.

Fundamental Analysis: Evaluation of a stock on the basis of its earnings, assets, profit margins, dividends, growth, and investment stature.

Growth Stock: The stock of a company whose sales, earnings, and net worth are expanding at an unusual rate. (The real honey, or "hulk," of stock picks.)

Hedger: An investor who enters the market with the specific intent of protecting an existing position in an underlying investment (instrument). (Better safe than sorry.)

Inside Track: Access to knowledge of goings on within a company and its stock and of their true meaning.

Insider: Technically anyone owning more than 5 percent of the stock of a public company, who must report to the SEC each month any substantial changes in holdings; also the term for members of management, board of directors, and other persons that possess material knowledge of the company's business prior to public disclosure.

Insider Selling: When management, board of directors, employees, and major shareholders are selling. (The rats are jumping ship!)

Insider Trading: Illegal profiting from privileged knowledge of an event or company business.

Institutional Investor (Investing): Generally speaking, any organization controlling the investment of megadollar pools of money. Purchase and sale of securities by mutual, endowment, or pension funds; banks; and insurance companies. (Sheep [herd] investing—often wrong and unwieldy.)

Interest: The price, or rental, paid for the use of money; usually stated in percentage per annum.

In-the-Money Option: An option that could be exercised and immediately closed out against the underlying instrument for a cash credit. A call option is in the money if the underlying market is above the call option's exercise price or below a put option's exercise price.

Intrinsic Value: As the difference between a stock's market price and its exercise price, the amount an option buyer would receive upon exercise of the option. Only call options with an exercise price below the market and put options with an exercise price above the market price have intrinsic value.

Investment Retirement Account (IRA): A tax-sheltered plan permitting deductions (up to $2,000 annually) to build a retirement income at age 59½ or later. (Too good to last.)

Junk Bond: High-yielding bond rated BB or below, or not rated at all. (What you see is what you get—high yield, high risk.)

Keogh Plan: Tax-sheltered pension plan for self-employed people.

Leverage Buying: Using other people's money (OPM) to generate earnings or gain, as when large amounts of senior debt securities exist in a corporate capitalization, ahead of its common stock. Other examples: using borrowed money to buy stocks, buying a house with a mortgage.

Liabilities: Any and all claims against a company.

Liquidation: Nervous selling by those who overstayed a bull market. (Too late!)

Liquidity: The capability of an investment to be converted quickly into cash. (Always provide for a quick getaway.)

Listing: Scheduling corporation securities for trading on an exchange. (Full of sound and fury, signifying nothing.)

Long: Position of owning (holding) a specific stock, bond, or futures contract.

Margin: The sum of money or value of securities actually deposited with a broker to purchase securities; designed to enable an investor to buy more securities than that person's own resources would permit. Margin requirements (currently 50 percent of the securities purchased) are determined at intervals by the Federal Reserve Board. (Don't invest beyond your means.)

Margin Call: A broker's demand for additional funds or collateral to protect security holdings that were purchased in part on borrowed money and have declined. (Time to pay the piper.)

Markup: The aggressive bidding up of prices. (Whoopee!)

New Issue: Initial public offering (IPO) of a security. ("Do you really want a virgin?")

New York Stock Exchange (NYSE): The major stock exchange in the United States. (Yawn.)

Odd Lot: A small amount of common stock, customarily less than 100 shares. (Small potatoes.)

Offer: A motion to sell at a specified price. (Good luck!)

Out-of-the-Money Option: An option that has no intrinsic value. For example, a call whose exercise price is above the underlying market price and a put whose exercise price is below the underlying market price. (Too bad.)

Outstanding Stock: Security issued and in public hands (ownership).

Over-the-Counter: A nationwide telephone and electronic market for securities not regularly traded on any exchange. (Often referred to as "under-the-counter" due to broker/dealer handling of stock prices and spreads between bid and offers.)

Paper Profit (Loss): Unrealized indicated gain (loss) on an investment position still held. (Don't count your stocks until they hatch.)

Penny Stock: Stock selling below $1. Often equated with a speculative or gamble character. (Penny stocks are unfortunately accompanied by unsophisticated investors unable to distinguish between relative value and a low stock price. Typically penny stocks trade in shark [penny stockbrokers]–infested waters.)

Per Share Net: For a given period (usually a fiscal year or fraction thereof), the total net earning of a company after taxes, divided by the number of common shares outstanding. (The standard yardstick.)

Preferred Stock: An issue of stock having a claim on assets and dividends of a company ahead of the common stock and usually entitled to dividends at a fixed rate. (A dinosaur!)

Premium: The amount by which a bond or preferred stock sells above its face amount (denomination) or a new issue sells above its offering price. Also, the price of an option.

Price/Earnings Ratio (P/E): The stock price divided by per share earnings of a company for the most recent or forecast twelve-month period; also called the "P/E multiple." (Another yardstick.)

Prime Rate: The interest rate charged by banks to their best customers on unsecured loans. (A myth for the average company.)

Principal Transaction: A transaction in which dealers (brokerage firms) buy and sell for their own account. In such transactions the customer sells or buys net from the dealer; the trade is without commission as the dealer profits or loses from the spread (difference between dealer cost and the transaction price) in lieu of a commission. (Watch yourself! The brokers are dealing for themselves.)

Put Option: A contract in which the seller gives the buyer the right, but not the obligation, to sell a specified stock, commodity, or financial instrument at a fixed price on or before a specified date; should the buyer (holder) wish to exercise this option, the seller assumes the obligation of taking delivery of the underlying stock or instrument. (For the cautious pessimist.)

Quotation: Naming the last sale and/or the highest bid and lowest offer prices as an indication of the market value of a security at a given point in time.

Red Chip: A relatively abandoned term to identify a less than "blue chip"-quality stock.

Securities and Exchange Commission (SEC): A federal organization for the regulation of the securities industry. (Stock cops.)

Security: The generic term for all marketable financial instruments.

Selling Short (Short Sale): Selling short is selling or offering to sell a security you do not own. Short sellers are bearish on the issues they sell short; they expect the share price to decline. So they borrow shares to sell (usually from a broker) with a view to selling at today's price and buying them back in the future at a lower price, at which time they deliver the borrowed stock and pocket the difference between their sale price and the purchase price. (In other words, selling short is a transaction in reverse order, enabling investors to profit from the decline in value of stocks they don't own. The American dream!)

Selling Short (Short Sale) Against the Box: A method by which investors can maintain a position in a stock even though they fear it will suffer a price decline. This is accomplished by selling short the stock as opposed to an outright sale of the stock owned. Should the stock price decline, the investor can purchase shares in the open market to be delivered against the borrowed shares sold, providing a short-term profit to compensate for the loss in value of the long position. (Usually these transactions are undertaken for tax purposes—that is, where the cost of the position is sooooo low as to make the tax burden more onerous than normal.) Conversely, if the stock moves up in value rather than down, the borrowed stock can be purchased in the open market and delivered, with a resulting loss, or the stock held (referred to as the "box") against which the short sale was made may be delivered in repayment of the borrowed shares. (A bit like having your cake and eating it too.)

Sell Off: Sharp decline in securities prices, either denoting a pause or the end in a bull market. (Not a pleasant experience for investors in a long position but absolute heaven for those who are "short.")

Share (Stock Certificate): A certificate representing ownership in the equity of a corporation. (Note: the stock certificate may be an endangered species; efforts are under way to eliminate it and reduce all stock ownership to "book entries"—literally an electronic bookkeeping entry. Scares us!)

Shareholder Record Date: The date of record that a shareholder must own stock to be entitled to dividends and to vote at the annual shareholder meeting.

Speculation: The employment of funds and assumption of risks primarily to create capital gain rather than income. In other words, every transaction where you aspire to buy low and sell high is something of a speculation!

Stock Dividend: A dividend paid in stock. For example, a 10 percent stock dividend declared for a 1,000-common shareholder would result in 100 new shares being issued to the shareholder. Here now occurs an interesting and baffling phenomenon: Most shareholders believe that they are receiving an item of value—additional ownership in the company. Nothing could be further from the truth. Since every shareholder receives 10 percent more shares, the percent of ownership remains unchanged. (The entire exercise is the equivalent of window dressing or paperhanging.) Nevertheless, stock dividends are much desired by shareholders, who apparently don't understand them or who still believe that you can get something for nothing. In some instances, the widespread belief in the value of stock dividends becomes a self-fulfilling prophecy, and the stock actually rises in price with the declaration of a stock dividend and in anticipation of the shareholder record date.

("There are stranger things on heaven and earth, Horatio, than you or I have dreamt of." The only true purpose of a stock dividend, other than the company avoiding paying a hard cash dividend, is to increase the number of shares in the public hands in order to improve liquidity and "float.")

Stock Split: Increasing the number of outstanding shares in a company by dividing the existing ones. For example, a two-for-one split doubles the number of shares outstanding and held by shareholders. (Commentary? See *Stock Dividend*. Ditto.)

Street Name: Stock held in the name of a broker or nominee instead of the legal owner. (Low profile.)

Technical Analysis: Evaluation of stocks on the basis of their recent market performance, volume, and price trends. See *Charts*.

Thin Market: Market in which trading is infrequent, with wide inside spreads between bid and offers. (Be careful. Getting in may be a breeze; getting out, a killer!)

Ticker: The electronic device that immediately reports and transmits, on tape, prices and volumes of security transactions. (The heartbeat of the market.)

Treasury Bills: Short-term (usually no longer than six months), interest-bearing obligations of the U.S. government. (How Uncle Sam pays the bills.)

Underwriter: Investment firm offering an issue of securities to the public. See *New Issue.*

Warrant: The right to buy a share or fractional share of a company's stock at a stated price and within a specified time limit; the subscription price is what you must pay to buy the shares, and the termination date is when the privilege expires. Sometimes warrants are registered and may trade in the public market alongside common stocks and other securities.

Yield: The return on investment in a given security at its current price, expressed as a percentage; calculated as the present indicated annual dividend divided by the market price of a single share.

THE LANGUAGE OF ORDER PLACING

OK, you've zeroed in on that special person. Just how are you gonna get that date? What you say and how you say it will set the stage. No matter how smooth you think you are and how nonchalant you wish to appear, you'll screw it up unless you give it some thought. Anyone "on the prowl" will do just that. He or she will wait for the right moment, try to say the right things, dress specially, and make the approach carefully.

Gawd! What we go through just to get a date . . . and maybe more! Well, the sex drive is important, but then again so is the money drive. Spend the same time necessary to move in on your capital gain trophies as you would on your libido trophies, and your investment performance will improve along with your sex life.

You're ready to make your move. You have made up your mind and are eager to enter an order with the broker. You're ready to buy, ready to sell. Now the easy part, right? Just call in the order, sit back and wait for the confirmation, pay the bill, collect the proceeds—

whatever. Wrong! The importance of choosing a reputable broker has been mentioned earlier, but that doesn't mean you should abdicate the investment process to that broker. There are many ways to enter an order. If it's not done properly, that poor execution could add to the cost of your purchase or detract from the net proceeds of a sale. You should no more carelessly throw out a transaction instruction to a broker than you should thoughtlessly and tactlessly approach that dynamite gal or guy for a date.

Dealing with the opposite sex is always complicated. Order placing is also complicated. Here are the most common ways to place orders.

All-or-None (AON) Order: An order that must be filled in its entirety or not at all.

Contingency Order: An order that will become effective only upon the fulfillment of some condition in the marketplace.

Day Order: An order in effect only until the closing of business that day.

Fill-or-Kill (FOK) Order: An order that must be filled immediately and in its entirety. Otherwise the order will be canceled.

Good till Canceled (GTC), or Open, Order: An order that remains in force until instructions to the contrary are issued. Not a wise move in a volatile stock; events may change dramatically, and the order could be "picked off" to the detriment of the investor.

Immediate-or-Cancel (IOC) Order: An order that must be filled immediately or it will be canceled; need not be filled in its entirety.

Limit Order: Order restricted to a specific price at which the trade may be executed; not to be confused with stop orders and stop-limit orders. A *buy limit* *order* instructs the broker to purchase the stock at a specified market price; the investor wishes to buy stock only if it trades at the price he or she wants. For example, an investor who wishes to buy at $35 a stock trading at 40 would place a buy limit order at $35. If the stock should drop to the 35, the trade would be executed (depending upon the amount of shares traded at that price and the number of orders in line ahead of it). Another example of a buy limit order would be an investor wishing to purchase the same stock at 40 maximum. The order would be entered to buy at 40. If there is enough stock trading at the 40 level, the order would be executed. In this example, the buy limit order prevents the purchase at a higher price, which could happen with a market order should the stock tick up. Using the same stock, the investor wishing to sell above the market would place a *sell limit order* at 45. An investor wishing to sell at the market would place a sell limit order at 40. Typically sell limit orders are placed above the current market price and buy limit orders below.

The broker may exceed the limit order only to the client's benefit. For example, a limit order to sell at a price of 40 may be executed at a higher price if market conditions provide an opportunity. However, the stock cannot be sold at a price below the limit. On the buy side of a limit order, the broker may pay less than the limit but not more.

If you want to have a limit order executed, you must enter it at a realistic price, not at a level too far out of line with the market.

Market Order: An order to be filled immediately— an order to buy or sell a stock at the prevailing market price, whatever that may be; the most popular and widely used order. Unsophisticated investors assume that the last sale reported or the current bid or offer is the "market" price they get when placing the order. This isn't necessarily true. Because markets change second by second, a market order to buy may be filled at a higher price and, conversely, a market order to sell may be carried out at a lower price. This is particularly true in over-the-counter and thinly traded issues. So, unless there is a compelling reason to "buy in at any price" or "get out at any price," it is not wise to place market orders.

Market-if-Touched (MIT) Order: A contingency order that becomes a market order if a security trades at a specified price. This order is entered at a price other than the current market price. A buy market-if-touched order is entered at a price below the current market, and a sell MIT order at a price above. When the security trades at the specified price, the broker will complete the order at the best price possible.

Not-Held Order: A market order that allows the broker flexibility in timing the execution—the discretion to move immediately or wait out the market to fill the order.

One-Cancels-the-Other Order: Really two orders in one, generally for the same security; instructs the broker to fill whichever order can be filled first and then cancel the remaining order. Uncommonly used and then typically in a fast-moving market, this setup prevents investors from making more trades than they are willing to, particularly in the same security. For example, it would be used if an investor wishes to either purchase a stock at 40 or sell at 45.

Specific-Time Order: Gives specific timing instructions beyond the day order or good-till-canceled order. For example, an order may be placed for execution at around market close or at some other specific time.

Stop-Limit Order: A contingency order to buy or

sell at a limit price or better if the security trades at a specified price; turns into a limit order when a stock trades at the price specified.

Stop-Loss Order: A contingency order to buy or sell a security at the current market price if the security trades at a specified price.

Stop Order: An order that instructs a broker to buy or sell a security once a price threshold is achieved. At that price the stop order becomes a market order, and the transaction takes place at whatever price the market offers. Stop sell orders must be entered at a price below the current market price; stop buy orders must be entered at a price above the current market price. Stop orders are sometimes referred to as "stop-loss orders" because they are often used to stop losses or to protect profits.

FINANCIAL BUZZWORDS AND IRREVERENT WALL STREET TERMINOLOGY

Webster's New Collegiate Dictionary is somewhat cynical in its definition of *buzzword*: "an important-sounding technical word or phrase often of little meaning used chiefly to impress laymen." We are inclined to be more gentle and forgiving in our perception of the buzzword phenomenon; we define it and its use as one-word solutions, simple and confident pronouncements, shorthand wisdom, and capsules of truth. On Wall Street we use buzzwords to provide a convenient focus for summations of business wisdom.

Throughout this book, we've spoken of the similarities of passion in human relationships and the money game on Wall Street. The accompanying emotions such as love (greed), hate (fear and loathing), elation (a high), depression (a downer), excitement (fad/infatuation), and so forth, all have spawned a string of potent expressions to present epoch-making concepts. These expressions, a wealth of jargon, have become Wall Street buzzwords.

Buzzwords alter the landscape of heretofore accepted vocabulary. Some endure to gain acceptance as legitimate business expressions; some even make it into the dictionary! Want an example of a few extreme cases? OK, try this on. Way back when, the expression "hot pants" was used to describe the character of a young woman in terms neither she nor her parents would appreciate; later it became a major fashion happening, broadly advertised by the very best of the retail trade and spoken of openly in fashion-conscious circles. Another? Try the word *coke*. A fuel and soft drink in past times, now an illegal narcotic.

On Wall Street, understanding buzzwords—or, if you prefer, streetspeak—may be important to your dealing with members of the financial community. Also on Wall Street, words may not always mean what they seem. In some cases the game hasn't changed, only the name. In others a familiar old name still prevails, but the underlying game has changed. So here we present those most used that have meaning for the investor. Pay attention, it's important.

Account Executive: Euphemism for "broker." Investors hear a lot of stuff from people who try to sell them stock. These people used to be called brokers, but apparently the title has been out of favor for some time now. It either isn't grandiose enough or carries too many negative connotations—a legacy from market crashes when customers couldn't even raise their brokers on the phone. Other euphemisms: financial consultant, investment executive, financial planner, and the old standby, registered representative. But if it looks like a broker, walks like a broker, speaks like a broker, then chances are it is a broker!

Baitback: A procedure whereby, if a stock has gained 150 percent, you sell half the position and hold the remainder.

Bottom Line: Net profits or the final conclusion.

Cigar Butt Approach: An investment approach analogous to a cigar butt found on the street that has only one puff left. It may not offer much of a smoke, but the bargain purchase price will make that puff all profit.

Cockroach Theory: Never is there just one cockroach in the kitchen: the first earnings disappointment is never the last.

Disneyland East: Euphemism for federal agencies, particularly the SEC.

Downsizing: The shrinking of an organization or company due to poor or hard times; indicates harsher times to come for the company and the stock. If you are an employee, downsizing usually translates into layoffs.

Globalization: The worldwide integration of economies and financial markets.

Going Public: Selling stock to the public for the first time.

Golden Handcuffs: A contract between a company and selected executives that provides irresistible financial incentives for loyalty. Lifetime employment, American style.

Golden Parachute: An extremely generous package of financial benefits granted to selected senior management in the event of a hostile takeover. American-style corporate entrepreneurialism.

Greenmail: The transaction whereby the company buys out (pays off) a major shareholder (hostile takeover threat), usually at a substantial profit for the hostile. Compare to blackmail.

Hands-On Manager: A working executive in touch with his company's people and business pulse. Very rare and very positive.

Hypermarket: Runaway stock market on the upside. A stock market on steroids.

In Play: The company, and consequently the stock, is being raided or seeking to sell out.

Institutional Imperative: Unseen force causing an institution to resist any change in its current direction; results in the herd investment policies of the institutional investor.

Kiting: Pumping up the stock price.

Lazarus Stock: A destroyed stock that has made a comeback. Taken from the biblical story of Lazarus, the brother of Mary and Martha, who was raised by Jesus from the dead (2 John).

Level Playing Field: A dreamer's belief that with proper and full disclosure all investors will be on an equal footing with one another. Never happen!

Leveraged Buyout: The ultimate OPM (other people's money) transaction: using borrowed funds a group takes ownership of a company. As many of these transactions do not work as do; the burden of debt service and repayment can crush a company. Be careful.

Loose Cannon: An unpredictable individual more likely to cause damage than not; the sole survivor among the similar phrases "unguided missile" and "accident waiting to happen." This buzzword actually made it into Webster's dictionary last year.

Major Technical Correction: A market crash! Stockbroker's way of avoiding the dreaded "C" word.

Market Breadth: A measure of market strength taken by measuring what kinds of stock are advancing, how many stocks are climbing, and how much trading volume is propelling the advance. In general the greater the breadth of a market rally, the longer it lasts and the farther it goes. So Wall Street pays a lot of attention to breadth, seeking to determine if a rally will persist or turn out to be a flash in the pan.

Married Put: The simultaneous purchase of a put option and a position in the market for the underlying instrument.

Maximize Shareholder Value: The cliché used to announce that the subject company is up for sale. See *In Play*.

Meltdown: Market crash complete with breakdown of communication and market liquidity. Example: October 1987 crash.

Naked: A long or short market position with no offsetting hedge.

Networking: Unashamed use of friends and contacts for personal gain.

Nondecision: Best defined by an example: when in doubt about selling a position (mental constipation), make a nondecision—sell some.

Outsourcing: Use of outside source suppliers for product components and services; often a euphemism for layoffs.

Permanently Altered Market Landscape: The aftermath of market crash! See *Major Technical Correction*.

Poison Pill: A management full-employment act and/or security blanket. A means by which a hostile takeover may be prevented by issuing securities to dilute a raider thereby entrenching management.

Profit Recession: A decline in corporate profits despite an increase in gross national product (GNP). We love this one! Is there any other kind?

Program Trading: Use of computers, and the new forms of trading that have evolved in tandem with their use; believed by many to have triggered 1987's "Black

Monday" and is a major factor in today's market volatility.

Restructuring: Recasting the company, a prelude to wholesale layoffs.

Ruler Stocks: Growth stocks that deliver relatively stable earnings growth through a deceleration of the economy. A fairy tale.

Soft Landing/Soft Peak: A recession occurring without significant consumer retrenching and/or business inventories liquidations. Another fairy tale.

Strips, Straps, Straddles, and Spreads: Burlesque-conjuring terms that describe various option plays—a subject not covered in this text and best left to the full-time professional. Otherwise you're gonna get your clock cleaned!

Sweetener: Something added in an underwriting (financing) to make a security more attractive; usually a warrant or a conversion privilege.

Tin Parachute: A package of benefits granted to selected key employees to provide some financial benefits in the event of a hostile takeover; less generous than the golden parachute. Compared to a golden parachute, a tin parachute is a free fall with an umbrella!

Value Investing: Formerly the term for purchasing undervalued stocks with good future propects, it may now refer to buying downtrodden companies worth more dead than alive. A time-honored investment strategy that no longer means what it once did.

Epilogue
Think Dirty—Live Clean
(Lust Without Guilt on Wall Street)

Most of us live vicariously, in one form or another. It may be through movie stars, athletes, or others whose lifestyles, accomplishments, or other enviable traits and/or actions we emulate—at least in our fantasies. Similarly we look at our sexual opposites in a reserved and socially acceptable manner, while all the time the mind's eye indulges in somewhat more titillating visions. These vicarious fantasies often provide the basis for our real-life motivation. Properly directed aspirations for wealth (financial success), sex (marriage and family), achievement (career fulfillment), prestige (peer recognition and social status), and leadership (community involvement) are generally acknowledged as healthy, positive forces.

Investing in the market is no exception. It's fine (and fun!) to think dirty and to indulge in fantasies about amassing great wealth in a single stroke, trading on infallible hot tips, "knowing" that frozen hog belly futures are just about to move limit up for five days in a row. It is the stuff of dreams! The point is, though, that it just isn't real. What *is* real is the possibility of achieving very substantial financial success in your investing program over time. And best of all, you can have the fun and enjoy the satisfaction, *without* putting yourself at unnecessary risk, if you apply the commonsense concepts of "clean living" we have outlined in this book. So that's really the final word: Think Dirty . . . but Live Clean!

About the Authors

Van William Knox III is president of Van William Knox, Inc., a registered investment advisory firm located in Chatham, New Jersey. Originally founded to meet the specific needs of an international clientele, his firm works with individual, profit sharing, pension, and retirement accounts in the United States, Europe, and Latin America.

Following his graduation in 1963 from Princeton University and a twenty-one-year career in the international pharmaceutical industry both here and abroad, Mr. Knox founded his present company in 1985.

Mr. Knox contributed to *The Individual Investor's Guide to Winning on Wall Street*.

Peter J. DeAngelis, CFA, is president of PDA Associates, Inc., a New Jersey management and financial consulting firm, and chairman of DOWBEATERS®, a registered investment advisory service.

He holds an M.B.A. from the New York University Graduate School of Business and has more than thirty years of experience in the investment field as a security analyst, research director, economist, and money manager. Mr. DeAngelis, a Chartered Financial Analyst, is past president of the nation's largest professional group of analysts, the New York Society of Security Analysts. He is author of *The Individual Investor's Guide to Winning on Wall Street* and coauthor of *The $2 Window on Wall Street* and *When to Sell Stocks and Pin Down Your Profits.*